Confirmation: Origins and Reform

Aidan Kavanagh

Confirmation:
Origins and Reform

Pueblo Publishing Company

New York

Design: Frank Kacmarcik

Printed in the United States of America

ISBN: 0-916134-88-1

In memory of
Ralph Keifer
and
Niels Krogh Rasmussen
R.I.P.

Contents

Introduction   ix

Abbreviations   xiii

Origins

CHAPTER ONE
The Place and Function of Liturgical Dismissals   3
1. *The Apostolic Tradition of Hippolytus*   5
2. *Eastern Evidence*   8
    a. *The Canons of Laodicea*   8
    b. *The Apostolic Constitutions*   10
    c. *Egeria's Travels*   12
3. *Ambrose, Augustine, and the West*   14
4. *Monastic Missae*   20
5. *Communion Dismissals: Prayers of Inclination*   27
6. *Summary*   31

CHAPTER TWO
A Baptismal *Missa*   39
1. *The Apostolic Tradition*   41
2. *Innocent I, Consignation, and Confirmation*   52
3. *New Perspectives*   65
4. *Origins of Confirmation*   69

Reform

CHAPTER THREE
The Reform of Confirmation   81
1. *The Initiatory Reform in General*   82

2. *The Reform of Confirmation* 89
   a. Divinae Consortium Naturae *of Paul VI* 90
   b. *The Question of Age* 97
3. *Problems and Estimates* 101

Bibliography 123

Index 129

Introduction

When I wrote *The Shape of Baptism: The Rite of Christian Initiation* a decade ago I avoided the matter of confirmation as much as possible because another volume in Pueblo Publishing Company's series, "The Reformed Rites of the Catholic Church," was planned to deal with that sacrament and its liturgy. That book, Gerard Austin's *Anointing with the Spirit. The Rite of Confirmation: The Use of Oil and Chrism*, appeared in 1985 as Volume III of the series, serving it well as a highly competent review of postconciliar reforms not only in the Roman Catholic but other churches as well.

I am particularly grateful for Austin's work because it allows me now to write about confirmation in ways that are more speculative. What follows represents my own research into the origins of confirmation and summary thoughts on its recent reform. The reader may not go too far wrong in regarding it as an extended footnote, an admiring gloss, to Austin's book.

The attentive reader may notice one thing which my research here set forth has made clear to me since I wrote *The Shape of Baptism*. I no longer think that the bishop's "confirmation prayer" in the earliest version we have of it, the Verona palimpsest translation into Latin of Hippolytus's *Apostolic Tradition*, was an epiclesis of the Holy Spirit. The conventional view of scholars is that it was, and I followed this reading in *The Shape of Baptism*. My reasons for rejecting this now will be found in the first two chapters of the present book. If I am right about this (as it appears Lampe was thirty years ago), the result is to shift the emphasis on the giving of the Holy Spirit away from what would later be called "consignation" and "confirmation" toward baptism itself and the eucharist, at least in this precursor document of the Roman initiatory tradition. Here I attempt to account for this reading of the text in terms of the specific liturgical structure occurring after baptism within which the text was used. I suggest that this liturgical structure was what is technically known as a dismissal, a *missa*, and that the structure we today know as "confirmation" originated here.

I use this suggestion as a working hypothesis in chapter three against which to review the 1971 reform of confirmation from the standpoint of this sacrament's origins and tortuous history, a reform which is remarkably radical when it comes to the structure, matter, and form of the sacrament. I conclude that with this reform a sacrament which began in one liturgical structure of the third century, a dismissal, has ended in another liturgical structure, a postbaptismal chrismation, with curious if not anomalous results. Thus the long history of this rite, which is filled with constant change and reinterpretation, continues unabated in its wandering course. One reason for this, I maintain, is that we have never had an adequate grasp of the rite's origins in light of its liturgical evidence as distinct from what the interpretations of theologians suggest, at various times, its meaning might be. Confirmation's origins are the burden of this book.

Hypotheses should be undertaken reluctantly and only when no other course in research appears fruitful. My own reluctance in venturing the hypothesis of confirmation's origins contained here is overcome by the absence of more compelling suggestions. More important, however, I sense that not grasping the origins of things leads ultimately to their misuse. A fuel pump functions poorly as a carburetor. Confirmation is a fundamentally modest rite which, positioned between baptism and eucharist, is capable of doing vast damage in the Church's initiatory economy if misperceived and misused. Confusion about it today suggests that we are unclear first about its origins, then about its use.

It is my hope that this book may be some small help in attaining a clearer picture of the sometimes perplexing richness and diversity of the initiatory polity of the Church Catholic past and present.

Aidan Kavanagh, O.S.B.
The Divinity School
Yale University
Solemnity of St. Benedict
1987

Abbreviations

AC	*Apostolic Constitutions*
AT	Hippolytus, *The Apostolic Tradition*
Botte	B. Botte, *La Tradition Apostolique de saint Hippolyte*
CCL	*Corpus Christianorum Latina*
CL	*Constitution on the Liturgy Sacrosanctum Concilium*
CSEL	*Corpus Scriptorum Ecclesiasticorum Latinorum*
Cuming	G.J. Cuming, *Hippolytus: A Text for Students*
Dix	G. Dix, *The Apostolic Tradition of St. Hippolytus of Rome*
LQF	*Liturgiewissenschaftliche Quellen und Forschungen*
Mansi	J.D. Mansi, *Sacrorum Conciliorum Nova et Amplissima Collectio*
OCA	*Orientalia Christiana Analecta*
PG	J.P. Migne, *Patrologia Graeca*
PL	J.P. Migne, *Patrologia Latina*
RB	*The Rule of Benedict*
RCIA	*The Rite of Christian Initiation of Adults*
The Rites	*The Rites of the Catholic Church, vol. 1*
RM	*The Rule of the Master*
Schaff-Wace	*A Select Library of Nicene and Post-Nicene Fathers of the Christian Church*
SC	*Sources Chrétiennes*
Whitaker	E.C. Whitaker, *Documents of the Baptismal Liturgy*

Origins

Chapter One

The Place and Function of Liturgical Dismissals

In a recent article I suggested that what is now called
confirmation may have originated as a dismissal which
concluded the service of baptism. I pointed out that if
this were the case then confirmation at its genesis
would have functioned in a way that is unfamiliar in
our usual discourse about this sacrament. If confirmation originated as a liturgical dismissal, I argued, it
would have functioned in respect of water baptism
and its anointing much as did any other dismissal in
respect of the service of worship it formally concluded, be it a eucharistic Word service, an office of
psalmody and prayer, or a catechumenal instruction
(which in the early church seems to have been more
worshipful than didactic in a modern classroom
sense). I noted that such dismissals may be said to
"complete" the services they ended in the sense that
they added nothing new or beyond the services themselves except a structural apolysis or formal conclusion. Thus when it is said that confirmation is the
"completion" or "perfecting" of baptism we might be
aware that there was a time when this meant not that
baptism was deficient in some respect. It meant something structural which would only later be filled with
theological meaning having to do with Holy Spirit, maturity, the fullness of initiation, and such like.[1]

All this depends, of course, on whether or not confirmation can be shown plausibly to have begun its com-

plicated and controverted life in the West as a baptismal dismissal. In this chapter and the next I wish to
expand the argument as to the retrievable facts, their
possible interpretation, and implications not only
touching confirmation but the larger question of how
dismissals affect the liturgy itself. The facts at issue are
those concerning the existence, form, and function of
the dismissal as a liturgical unit in the evolution of
Christian worship. This in itself presents an initial difficulty because liturgical dismissals have never received
a unified or magisterial study by scholars. Dismissals
have instead been treated mainly during the course of
studies of some larger structure such as the eucharist,
penance, or certain offices. Often they are mentioned
and documented (but not always) in passing, without
much comment on their form and function within the
liturgy as a whole.

Yet we know from patristic allusions that dismissals
often took a lot of time, something which suggests itself hardly at all when one looks only at the texts to
be said on their occasion without considering the ritual logistics of dealing with the numbers, often large,
of those being dismissed and the effects of this on the
entire worshiping assembly.[2] The amount of movement involved in dismissing numbers of people—
catechumens, penitents, energumens, non-
communicating faithful, and finally the entire
assembly— must have occasioned extensive shifting
and reallocation of the assembly's clergy and people.
Such activities increased in scope as congregations
grew in size during and after the fourth century,and
came later to include also processions of entry, of
transferring gifts to the altar, and of communion. People did what they had to do in getting from one place
to another, and clergy did what they could to direct
such movement lest it turn rowdy and disedifying in
large spaces without aisles defined by blocks of

4

immoveable pews. Such events resisted not only rubrical constraint but also catechetical admonition. Eutychius, patriarch of Constantinople in the late sixth century, preached that "they act stupidly" who teach the people to sing Psalm 23. 7–10 during that procession with the gifts to the altar (which would later be called the Great Entrance) because the text refers to the "King of Glory" being brought in. Eutychius points out that it is only later that prayer and supplications will render the gifts something more than bread and wine. Eutychius did not prevail over popular piety; Nicholas Cabasilas felt it necessary to make the same point c. 1350, even though the Cherubikon hymn at the Great Entrance, with its "King of All," had by then become standard and deeply traditional.[3]

In examining dismissal texts one must keep in mind that rite is action and involves more than things said. Thus as we review the texts of dismissals we shall try to evoke something of the ritual logistics which accompanied the things said during the events in prayer.

1. THE APOSTOLIC TRADITION OF HIPPOLYTUS
The earliest allusion to what is a formal dismissal protocol is in Hippolytus's conservative church order, the *Apostolic Tradition* (AT),c. 215–220. The context is catechumenal:

"When the teacher has finished giving instruction, let the catechumens pray by themselves, separated from the faithful. . .And when they have finished praying, they shall not give the Peace, for their kiss is not yet holy. . .After their prayer, when the teacher has laid hands on the catechumens, he shall pray and dismiss them. Whether the teacher is a cleric or a layman, let him act thus."[4]

In brief, after the instruction the catechumens pray privately for a while, perhaps kneeling or prostrate and more or less in silence. Then the instructor publicly lays hands on them, prays for them, and dismisses them. The entire instruction, which Hippolytus elsewhere suggests takes place "in the church,"[5] concludes with prayer, hand laying, and dismissal. Instruction ending in this fashion punctuates the catechumens' lives over a usual period of three years,[6] down to and including their final meeting as catechumens prior to their baptism. Here the bishop himself presides:

"On the Saturday those who are to receive baptism shall be gathered in one place at the bishop's decision. They shall all be told to pray and kneel. And he shall lay his hands on them and exorcize all alien spirits, that they may flee out of them and never return into them. And when he has finished exorcizing them, he shall breathe on their faces; and when he has signed their foreheads, ears, and noses, he shall raise them up. And they shall spend the whole night in vigil; they shall be read to and instructed. . .At the time when the cock crows, first let prayer be made over the water. . ."[7]

The procedure is closely similar to an ordinary instruction, but more solemn and with the bishop presiding instead of a mere catechist. The elect catechumens first pray. Then the bishop lays hands and prays for them, adding an exsufflation and signation. There is, however, no final word of dismissal since they are to be read to and instructed through the night until baptism commences before dawn with prayer over water. But the "dismissal" elements of prayer and hand laying, expanded by an exsufflation and signation (no doubt in the sign of the cross), remain as the act of one who presides.

This illustrates the versatility of the structure of prayer and hand laying as it has coalesced into different liturgical units by the early third century. Although there is often prayer without hand laying in AT, there is never hand laying without prayer, and hand laying with prayer is done only upon such persons as catechumens, major ministers, and the baptized. Indeed, so prominent is this structure that sections 3–14 of AT are called in the Greek *Epitome* text *peri cheirotonias* ("About Hand Layings") and deal with which ministries are to be ordained by prayer and hand laying (bishops, presbyters, and deacons) and which are not (confessors, widows, readers, virgins, subdeacons, and healers). In the whole work only major ministers and the eucharistic gifts are prayed for with epicleses invoking God to send the Holy Spirit.[8]

These combinations in various liturgical situations are anything but random. They are studied and consistent, as is suggested by AT's precision with regard to when hand laying is *not* to occur (with the lesser ministries) and when it *is* to occur (with major ministries and with catechumens even when the catechist is not a cleric). Given the diversity of the combinations of prayer and hand laying in AT it is obviously not possible to give only one answer to the question of what hand laying *by itself* means for Hippolytus. Yet given the patterned and disciplined use of prayer and hand laying in the document it may be possible to see in this usage an early stage in the development of a policy of liturgical "sealing" (*sphragis* in Greek, *signaculum* in Latin)—as when the kiss of peace concluding the prayers of the faithful or the Lord's Prayer comes to be called *signaculum orationis,* or when the final day of Lenten fasting (the Friday of the sixth week) comes to be called in Egypt the "seal of the fast."[9] All these may well be extensions of the practice of concluding liturgical prayer units with formulas such as the *hatima* (seal) of Jewish *berakoth,* the doxologies in Christian thanksgiving prayers from the New Testament and

Didache onward,[10] and the *ekphonesis*-doxology in Eastern practice.[11]

In view of all this we suggest that AT's dismissal rite of catechumens, involving prayer and hand laying by the senior person present, represents an early instance of the Christian instinct to "seal" a unit of worshipful activity by a final address of God in prayer and by physical contact with the presiding minister. The form would thus represent a liturgical *sphragis* or *signaculum* set upon a synaxis of worship by word and action.

To test this suggestion it will be necessary to pursue the dismissal's further formalization in subsequent sources, returning later to the liturgy of baptism in AT to ascertain whether there may be a dismissal structure there. The question now is whether there is evidence beyond AT for a further formalization and extension of the catechumenal dismissal structure found there.

2. EASTERN EVIDENCE
a. The Canons of Laodicea
This set of sixty canons is a collection of subjects dealt with in early fourth century synods and councils, including Nicaea (325) and an otherwise unknown assembly at Laodicea which may have met sometime between 345 and 365, over a century after AT was written. Canon 19 of this collection deals with how the eucharistic Word service ends:

"After the sermons of the bishops, the prayer for the catechumens is to be made first by itself; and after the catechumens have gone out, the prayer for those under penance; and after these have passed under the hand and departed, there should then be offered the three prayers of the faithful, the first to be said entirely in silence, the second and third aloud, and then the peace is to be given."[12]

Two groups, catechumens and penitents, are being dismissed. Each group is prayed for separately, suggesting that each prayer is designed to refer to a specific group. Who does the praying is not specified, nor is whose hand it is that members of each group are to pass under on their way out. Since at this time, however, the bishop was the regular presider at all public liturgical events there can be little doubt that it is he who prays and to his hand that the dismissed come. Only after the catechumens and penitents have departed may the prayers of the faithful begin. These seem to be a sequence of tripartite bidding prayers involving silent prayer first and then two prayers out loud. This suggests the prayer structure and assignment of prayer roles to deacon and bishop which we shall see detailed in the roughly contemporary *Apostolic Constitutions.* From that source we may surmise in this canon that after the silent prayer a deacon leads the assembly in vocal prayer for the same intention and then the bishop sums up the whole prayer of the assembly, both silent and vocal, in a collect-type prayer of his own. Then the whole tripartite form is repeated for other intentions as long as seems necessary.[13] Only after all this may the kiss of peace be exchanged, "and so the Holy Oblation is to be completed."

The prayers for catechumens and penitents on the other hand seem to be unipartite, unlike the prayers of the faithful. For catechumens and penitents the bishop may simply have said a single prayer for each group before the members passed individually under his hand and departed. But other more detailed sources such as *Apostolic Constitutions* and Egeria, as we shall see, report both the tripartite bidding structure for dismissals and the involvement of deacons. It may be that Laodicea is merely unspecific about this. But it cannot be ruled out that the tripartite bidding structure of prayer used by the faithful had not at that time been extended to the rites of dismissing catechumens and penitents. This would suggest a dismissal structure similar to what we have seen for catechumens in AT, which involved only a prayer for the catechumens with hand laying by the catechist and their dismissal.

That this contrasting euchology—unipartite for catechumens and penitents, tripartite for the faithful—is what Laodicea is talking about is made more likely given the policy in early sources of emphasizing the *differences* between catechumens and the baptized. Catechumens pray by themselves separately from the faithful, and they do not share the kiss of peace because their kiss is not yet holy (AT 18);[14] as they come close to baptism hands are laid on them daily "while they are exorcized" (AT 20);[15] catechumens at the agape meal (called "The Lord's Supper") do not receive blessed but exorcized bread and may not recline (*non concumbat*) at table along with the faithful (AT 26–27).[16] Laodicea may imply that neither do they have the same tripartite euchology said on their behalf as the faithful will use in their solemn prayers after the dismissals have taken place.

b. The Apostolic Constitutions (AC)
This work is a church order of Antiochean provenance, compiled c. 370–380 from a variety of earlier sources, including AT.[17] In its eighth book AC, like AT 4, gives rubrics and texts for the first eucharist of a newly ordained bishop beginning directly after the sermon.[18] Included are extensive rites for dismissing four groups: *catechumens,* who have not yet been elected for baptism; *energumens,* who are said to be possessed by

unclean spirits;[19] *illuminated*, who are senior catechumens already elected to receive baptism at its next public administration; and *penitents*, those guilty of sins serious enough to have disrupted the spiritual equilibrium and peaceful communion of faithful life in common. The Ninevites and the prodigal son are mentioned in the prayers themselves as types of these penitents.

Since Laodicea it seems that pastoral diagnosis has become more precise and liturgically elaborate. Not only does AC dismiss catechumens and penitents but energumens and a second category of catechumens, the illuminated, so called because only on their election to receive baptism were they allowed to hear and be instructed in the gospels, which were their "illumination." Also more precise in AC are the prayer roles of deacon, bishop, and faithful as well as prayer content and structure of the dismissal rites.

The dismissal structure is constant in AC for all four categories of persons being dismissed. Prayer is in tripartite bidding form, the content in each case being tailored to the group being dismissed. The structure is as follows:

1. *A deacon calls for prayer* and the group probably kneels or prostrates in silence for some time.

2. *The deacon leads an ektene* (litany) of some length for the group, to which everyone responds *kyrie eleison* after each petition. Toward the end of the ektene the group is told to stand up, bow down, and "receive a blessing," by which it meant. . .

3. *A lengthy prayer by the bishop*, asking God to help the group and concluding with a doxology. A Vienna manuscript of AC has a marginal note by a later hand entitling this prayer "laying on of hands."[20] When taken together with Laodicea 19 and the evi-

dence we shall see in Egeria it is probable that this episcopal prayer concluded with. . .

4. *The bishop laying his hand on each member of the group* as the group leaves at the deacon's command.

In each of AC's four dismissals we may see the developed liturgical and euchological structure which was adumbrated in AT's dismissal of catechumens: prayer by the group, prayer and hand laying by the presider, and dispersal of the group.

c. Egeria's Travels

Egeria was, it seems, a religious sister from southern Gaul or Spain who is known to have toured the Middle East as a pilgrim between 381 and 384. She was in Jerusalem for Lent and Easter of 383 and describes the liturgy there in her journal, about a third of which has survived, noting especially those things which struck her as different from what she had known at home. She was in Jerusalem contemporaneously with the composition of AC to the north around Antioch and perhaps at the end of or just after the episcopate of Cyril, the famous bishop and mystagogue of Jerusalem.[21]

Egeria is a sharp foreign eye and indefatigable reporter of what she saw in and around the Holy City. She notes, for example, the *kyrie eleison* response, screamed out over and over again by a choir of boys, and which she has to translate for her western readers as *miserere domine*. This suggests that the Greek response certainly, and perhaps even the litanic prayer structure to which it was attached, was new to her and unknown to her intended Western readers.[22] The litany and *kyrie* response concluded with a collect-like "prayer and commemoration of all" said by the bishop in connection with the dismissal at each of the three daily offices. This euchological structure Egeria describes is not fundamentally different from that we have seen in the dismissals of AC 8 and Laodicea 19.

She is precise and consistent in detailing the dismissals she witnessed in the liturgies of Jerusalem, but their presence seems not to surprise her. What does interest her seems to be the rich variety, complexity, and mobility of the liturgies in the Holy City and its environs, together with the choice of specific readings appropriate to a given liturgy's time and place of celebration. This interest on her part suggests that at home she had been used to a simpler and more provincial form of worship using a course reading (*lectio continua*) of the biblical books which was on the whole unrelated to time or place of celebration.

So far as the Jerusalem dismissals are concerned, she has a name for them, *missa*, and is already familiar with their place and use in the liturgy; she does not have to explain either the term or structure to her readers.[23] But the very complexity of Jerusalem usage, compared to her own, compels her to mention the dismissals no less than seventy-two times. She never clearly uses *missa* as a technical term for the eucharist, as would become general in Western parlance only well into the fifth century. For her *missa* means a formal unit of prayer and action which seals or marks off a preceding liturgical service of whatever sort, often from another one which follows immediately. When Egeria mentions a *missa* she has a definite ceremony in mind. *Fit oratio et missa* (37.7); *hoc autem lecto fit oratio, benedicuntur catechumeni, sic fit missa* (37.9); *facta ergo missa in ecclesia maiore, id est ad Martyrium* [the bishop's basilica on Golgotha], *deducitur episcopus cum ymnis ad Anastase* [the shrine of the tomb of the resurrection behind the basilica] *et ibi completis quae consuetudo est diebus dominicis fieri in Anastase post missa Martyrii* [i.e., the eucharist, which Egeria calls *offerre* or *oblatio*] (30.3).

Mohrmann observes that Egeria uses *missa* as a technical term denoting ". . .un rite final (ou une pluralité de rites) assez mal défini,"[24] a curious thing to say by so careful a reader of ancient texts. Egeria is in fact clear about what the Jerusalem *missa* entailed. All regular assemblies for worship end with a *missa*. Either a deacon (24.6–7) or the bishop himself (24.2) conducts prayers for individuals, mentioning names. To these petitions a choir of boys responds loudly each time *kyrie eleison*. At the end the bishop says a collect-type "prayer for all," sometimes called a "blessing." Then the dismissed, whether catechumens or faithful, come one by one to the bishop's hand (24.7).[25] Egeria is quite explicit about this for morning prayer (24.2), midday prayer (24.3), and *Lucernare* or vespers (24.4–7), where one can see the rite at its fullest. Mohrmann never mentions the dismissed coming to the bishop's hand, nor does she remark that the *missa* is something only the bishop does. Egeria says that even when the bishop is not present for an office he is sent for to come and perform its *missa* (24.3–4). This conforms with Laodicea 19 and AC 8, as we have seen, and is not out of keeping with AT 19, where it is the catechist who prays over, lays hands on, and dismisses his catechumens.

3. AMBROSE, AUGUSTINE AND THE WEST
Western liturgies at the end of the fourth and the beginning of the fifth centuries were probably not so complex as that which Egeria witnessed in the pilgrim-crowded city of the holy places. Nor did these Western liturgies have at that time reporters like Egeria to describe them in detail. Would that Rome, Milan, Hippo, and Alexandria had their own Egerias.[26] Western *liturgical* evidence at this period is not so abundant nor is it of Egeria's kind, which often tells us more about the actual mechanics of a liturgy than can be distilled from liturgical texts, canonical allusions, or

episcopal admonitions. References to *missa* in Western documents are thus less frequent and more terse, yet we know that the rite existed and that Egeria was already familiar with its structure and had a name for it before she arrived in Jerusalem.[27] She did not see something new in it, but only more of them than she was accustomed to at home.

Augustine, who became bishop of Hippo in North Africa in 395, says in Sermon 49.8: *post sermonem fit missa catechumenis, manebunt fideles.* His monastic contemporary Cassian tells the story of a monk who yearned *celebrare velut diaconum catechumenis missam (Institutes* 11.16). And while Western allusions such as these usually center on the dismissal of catechumens, they do not do so exclusively. Cassian also mentions a monastic office *missa*, as in the case of a monk who came late for common prayer: *ulterius oratorium introire non audet nec semet ipsum admiscere psallentibus, sed congregationis missam stans pro foribus praestolatur (Institutes* 3.7.1).

The *missa* structure is also evident in the case of penitents. Augustine complains twice about how long the line of penitents had been when he dismissed them from the liturgy with the "blessing."[28] There is no way to account for his complaint unless the long line was coming to his hand one by one, a time-consuming process especially if catechumens had earlier been dismissed similarly. Sozomen, an Easterner writing around 450, describes this same treatment of penitents at Rome with prayer and hand laying.[29] The public handling of penitents in the late fourth century seems to have taken place in *missa* form by the bishop, something we know about because of prohibitions against presbyters doing this.[30] Thus Pope Damasus (d. 384) in Epistle 5: *nec publice quidem in missa quemquam poenitentem reconciliare.* The second council of Carthage (390), canon 3, forbids presbyters *reconciliare quemquam publica missa.* The burden of both texts is to insist on the traditional prerogative of the bishop alone using the *missa* structure.

It is noteworthy that the word *missa*, as in the instances just mentioned, is rarely used in western sources for the dismissal or reconciliation of penitents with prayer and hand laying. More usual is the phrase "blessing of penance,"[31] even though the liturgical structure to which this refers is in fact a *missa* of prayer over the group and a coming under the bishop's hand by each penitent. This represents a formalization of title for two distinct uses of one and the same liturgical structure. It is called *missa* when catechumens and faithful are involved, and more usually a "blessing" when penitents are involved as in Augustine's sermon mentioned above.

There is both a theological and a liturgical foundation for this titular distinction between two sorts of *missae*. Theologically penitents are, despite the seriousness of sin, still baptized Christians. Even though their sin is of such proportions as to have attenuated their relationship to the worshiping community it has not wiped out their baptism. In this, at least, catechumens, who are not yet baptized, and penitents differ. Liturgical manifestations of this appear subtly in AC 8 where, after his litany and the bishop's collect prayer over the dismissed, the deacon bids catechumens, energumens, and the illuminated "Go forth (*proelthete*). . .in peace." But penitents he bids "Depart (*apoluesthe*)." The difference in imperatives may be significant; *proelthete* seems to suggest leaving the building:; *apoluesthe*, which might better be translated "withdraw," suggests that penitents, after coming to the bishop's hand, went to a special place in the church reserved for them where they were allowed to remain without communicating at the eucharist which followed. Penitents are thus, it seems, not asked to leave the building as are the unbaptized catechumens, but to withdraw into their own section at the rear or sides while those who will communicate proceed with the Oblation. In some churches, as we shall see, this dismissal of penitents took place just before communion.

The versatility of the *missa* structure is here once again in evidence. While the *structure* of episcopal prayer and hand laying remained stable, the *prayer content* varied in respect to different groups within the liturgical assembly, all of which resulted in locating differently these various groups within the liturgical celebrations. Liturgical sources are often precise on the location of different groups or "orders" of Christians—men and women, juniors and elders, magistrates, religious and clergy, penitents and catechumens—in specific places during worship services. The congregation was composed of distinct groups which were arranged corporately and could regard each other corporately during the services, especially when certain groups such as catechumens, penitents, and others were prayed for and then could be seen to come individually under the bishop's hand as they left the building or redeployed themselves within it. Although these arrangements are sometimes interpreted by modern authors as evidence of the liturgy's simply taking on social distinctions found in secular society of the time, the matter is more complicated than that and is more in line with the gospel than with secular custom. Although Christians were regarded as fundamentally one in faith and baptism (Galatians 3.27–29), the human condition remained richly diverse even among the baptized. Even the baptized possess different gifts (1 Corinthians 12), ministries (AT 2–14), and vocations (to marriage or ascetical celibacy). That such differences should not be formally recognized in the very deployment of the liturgical assembly never seems to have crossed anyone's mind, and it was one of the liturgy's chief functions to marshal all this diversity into a richly varied unity which transcended ordinary cultural or civic groupings.

As ways of dealing with catechumens and penitents became more standardized by the fifth century the importance and extent of dismissal structures grew, only to decline into vestigiality thereafter as catechumens decreased in number and as other, more private, ways of dealing with penitents came on the scene under monastic auspices. It became increasingly common in the West to allude to whole liturgical units, particularly the eucharist, as *missa* because of the extensiveness of the ceremonies this structure involved. Although Egeria, as we have seen, regularly uses old Western terms to refer to the eucharist, namely *offerre* and *oblatio*,[32] on two occasions (25.10 and 27.8) she may use *missa* in oblique reference to the eucharist proper.[33]

Ambrose of Milan, Egeria's contemporary, is probably the first clearly to give the eucharist as such the title *missa*. In a letter to his sister Paulina Ambrose reports what happened in Milan on Palm Sunday 385: "After the readings and sermon, having dismissed the catechumens, I performed the *traditio symboli* for some senior catechumens [*competentibus*] in the baptistery of the [Portiana] basilica." While doing this he was told that the church was surrounded by a mob incited by Arians. "I remained inside and began the Mass [*missam facere coepi*]. As I offered. . .I wept bitterly and prayed to God in this very oblation that he might allow no blood to be shed in *in causa ecclesiae*."[34] *Missam facere coepi* can mean nothing else here than the eucharist proper, beginning most likely with the bringing of the gifts to the altar.

Such terminological linkage between *missa* and the eucharist would not, however, become general in the West until a century later,[35] reflecting the impact which the developed dismissal ceremonies were having on the perceptions of ministers and people alike. Not all of these perceptions seem to have been without problems. In several of his surviving sermons Bishop Caesarius of Arles (c. 470–542) admonishes his people, and on occasion even clerics, not to leave the church after the readings and sermon, but to remain *donec divina mysteria compleantur.*[36] It seems that Caesarius is deploring the practice of many in the congregation using the occasion of the dismissals at the end of the Word service to mingle with the dismissed and leave the church along with them. This abuse no doubt afforded bishops of the time with one motive for suppressing the dismissals at this point in the Sunday service in order to remove the occasion for such disedifying exits. By the seventh century in Gaul an *Expositio* of the Gallican liturgy describes the dismissals in some detail, but the author makes clear that the rite was by then little more than a memory.[37] Yet the earlier existence of the *missa* structure was no less common in the West than in the East, with the possible exception of Rome itself.[38]

Jungmann does not think that there was ever a dismissal of catechumens at Rome, except at the great public scrutinies during Lent, because catechumens there were not allowed to attend the eucharist at all prior to their baptism.[39] In this connection one recalls the stipulations of AT that catechumens are not to pray with the faithful, exchange the kiss of peace with them, nor even recline with them at agape meals. The only dismissal AT contains for them is not from any public liturgical service but only from their own instruction sessions, as we have seen. Similarly catechumens are not prayed for in the fifth century *Deprecatio Gelasii,* a long litany sung at the beginning of the Roman eucharist, although neophytes and penitents are.[40] The implication is that catechumens are not

there to be prayed for. But catechumens *are* prayed for
in early allusions to the Roman prayers of the faithful.
In a fifth century appendix to a letter of Pope
Celestine I (d. 432) it is said that bishops and faithful
together say *obsecrationes sacerdotales* for unbelievers,
idolators, Jews, heretics, schismatics, penitents, and
catechumens. Felix II (d. 492) also mentions prayer for
presumably absent catechumens.[41] It is noteworthy by
contrast that in AC 8 the prayers of the faithful contain no intercessions for catechumens, energumens,
penitents, or the elect.[42] The reason is clear: these
have already been prayed for at their dismissals, something that was not the case in Rome. This evidence
tends to bear out Jungmann's contention.

4. MONASTIC MISSAE

The term *missa* is used in some early monastic texts in
a way similar to that which we have already seen in
Egeria. It may refer *first* to a dismissal ceremony; *second* to an office which is concluded by the *missa* ceremony of prayer and hand laying; *third* to the eucharist
in the Western sense of Mass. Sometimes the first and
second senses overlap in particular contexts. Cassian
(c. 360–435), that collector of monastic lore East and
West, refers to *missa* in the first and second senses but
not in the third. About a century later, however,
Cassiodorus, a man of affairs but with a monastic
bent, is using *missa* as a term for the eucharist with
some regularity; *missarum ordo, in sanctarum celebratione
missarum.*[43] Sixth century Western synods continue
this trend[44] at a time when dismissals in the eucharist
are, as we have seen, beginning to fall into disuse due
to abuses such as that mentioned by Caesarius of
Arles, to a decline in numbers of catechumens, and to
new ways of dealing with penitents.

But in monasteries old ways often are retained longer
than elsewhere. In the related sixth-century monastic

documents known as the *Rule of the Master* (RM) and the *Rule of Benedict* (RB)[45] the use of *missa* in the first and second senses (as in Cassian) is clear, but in the third sense disputed. In the "liturgical code" of both Rules (RM 33–49, RB 8–20), which lays out how the offices are to be said, the night offices and lauds conclude with only a litany, *id est kyrie eleison* (RB 9.10, 12.4), called *rogus dei* in RM (35.1, 44.4). But the other offices from prime through compline all end in what RB calls *missae*. In these six cases the office *missae* are preceded by the petitionary prayer of a litany, called *kyrie eleison*. At vespers this litany precedes the petitionary Lord's Prayer (RB 13.12, 17.8), and at compline the *missa* involves the litany and a "blessing" (RB 17.10). What are these *missae* which RB lists as the final act of all the day hours and compline?

At first glance neither RM nor RB appears to answer this question. That *missa* denotes in a general way that an office simply "concludes"[46] seems unlikely in view of the formulaic way statements are made in RB 17:

post expletionem vero trium psalmorum
recitetur lectio una, versus et kyrie
eleison et missas. (RB 17.4 for prime)

ternos psalmos, lectionem et versu,
kyrie eleison et missas. (RB 17.5 for terce, sext, none)

canticum de Evangelia, litania, et
oratione dominica fiant missae. (RB 17.8 for vespers)

versu, kyrie eleison, et benedictione
missae fiant. (RB 17.10 for compline)

Nor can Linderbauer's notion that *missae* here refers to the prayers of the monks being "sent off" to God be sustained.[47] More probably when RB in its liturgical code uses *missas* or *missae,* which are plural forms, it means something more definite than a general conclusion and something less fanciful than sending prayers off to God. Especially when a form of the verb *fieri* or *esse* is involved (as in *missae fiant*) or is understood by context, some sort of rite or ceremony is implied.[48] The phrase at compline, *benedictione missae fiant*, "the dismissals are done with blessing," is redolent of formal ceremony the content of which was not only prayer but some kind of action as well, as we have already seen in Egeria. This same redolent sense is preserved in the *ite missa est* of the Roman Mass today.

To clarify the ceremonial implications of *missae* in RB, and perhaps also of *rogus dei* in RM, two things are necessary. One must first be aware of liturgical tradition prior to the sixth century where, as we have seen in both Eastern and Western evidence, the regular form of dismissal at the end of a liturgical service was petitionary prayer by deacon and/or bishop and a coming under the bishop's hand. Secondly one must be able to infer details of the monastic *missa* from other allusions to it from within the monastic document itself. We have already noted how all the day offices end with *missae* as stipulated in RB 17, but these say nothing about the *missa* ceremony itself. Perhaps RB's directions concerning holy communion may help fill in the picture.

Monasticism until well after the sixth century was essentially a lay movement typified by prayer, celibacy, and asceticism, the last two being endeavors to which ordained clergy were not by office bound in all churches. For this reason one does not find in early monastic rules elaborate dispositions for eucharistic liturgy as one does for the liturgy of the hours. RM, however, provides for daily communion under both species from the reserved sacrament administered by the abbot, even though he is not *quis de ordine sacerdotum*. In RM communion took place, according to de Vogüé, between sext, none, or vespers (if it were a fast day) and the common meal.[49] Whatever this communion service involved, it was brief and contained the kiss of peace, suggesting that it was preceded by some form of petitionary prayer such as a collect, litany, or the Lord's Prayer. The eucharist as a whole seems to have been celebrated within the monastery only rarely, when outside clergy were present; on Sundays the monks apparently attended the nearest parish church.

Although RB admitted clergy to the community as members, like other monastic rules it does not know the eucharist within the monastery daily, but at most only on Sundays and a few feast days; nor is it entirely clear in RB that there was even daily communion. The term *communio* does, however, appear in RB three times, all of them outside the liturgical code. In 63.4 the monks are directed to approach (*accedant*) the kiss of peace and the *communio* according to their rank of seniority in the community. This suggests a communion procedure like that in RM, with overtones of processional movement (*accedant*). In 38.10 the table reader is to be given a drink of wine before he begins to read at the common meal "because of the Holy Communion," which would have kept him fasting until afterwards. This implies that communion took place immediately before the meal, at whatever time this occurred, and after the office preceding the meal—either sext at midday or none later in the afternoon (also RM 24.14). Finally in 38.2 the table reader is directed to enter upon his week of service by asking a blessing in the oratory on Sunday *post missas et communionem*. De Vogüé thinks the phrase means "after Mass and communion" since the day is Sunday. But de Bhaldraithe thinks that *missas* (plural) here may very well mean the end of sext because that is just how it is described in RB 17.5.[50]

De Vogüé's interpretation is not implausible, given the developing synecdoche in non-monastic sources of *missa* for the eucharist. On the other hand, however, it would represent the only instance in RB where the eucharist is called *missa*, and in the plural as *missae*. Indeed, the only other possible reference to eucharistic celebration, and it is even more oblique and problematic, concerns parents offering their son to the monastery by wrapping their petition and the boy's hand *cum oblatione. . .in palla altaris* (RB 59. 1–2, 8). *Oblatio* may mean the presentation of the gifts at a eucharistic celebration.[51] *Cum oblatione* may, however, refer to an offering in cash or kind for the boy's upkeep being presented by those parents who could afford it; the wrapping does not occur if the parents have nothing to give.

Since this text is oblique and disputably eucharistic,[52] it leaves *post missas et communionem* of 38.2 the only other putative reference to eucharistic celebration in RB. What is beyond dispute is that RB more consistently refers to the eucharist, as does RM and other contemporary and earlier monastic rules, in terms of *communion* from the reserved sacrament administered as a rule by the unordained abbot between the offices of sext or none (*post missas*) and the main meal. The communion service is thus bracketed in RB by office and *missa* before and the common meal afterward.

Further insight into what was involved might be seen in the words of RB 60.4 concerning the status of ordained clerics who are members of the monastic community. Although not wholly adverse to admitting clergy (as is RM 83, which calls them "outsiders"), RB 60. 1–3 is nonetheless reluctant: "do not agree too quickly," and make sure they realize that they will have ". . .to observe the full discipline of the rule without any mitigation."[53] Such clergy must, however, be accorded what is due their office as *quis de ordine sacerdotum*, by which RB means deacons, presbyters, and bishops as distinct from lesser ministers of the *gradus clericorum.*[54] The only outward sign of honor allowed such an ordained monastic is this: *Concedatur ei tamen post abbatem stare et benedicere aut missas tenere, si tamen iusserit ei abbas.*

This passage is usually translated: "He should, however, be allowed to stand next to the abbot, to give blessings and to celebrate Mass, provided that the abbot bids him."[55] Steidle thinks that *missas* here means office dismissals, as we have seen in RB 17.[56] Mohrmann translates it "Mass"[57] due to the phrase *missas tenere* in canon 21 of the Council of Agde (506), which speaks of *clerici. . .qui missas facere aut tenere voluerit.* But her argument loses force with the term *clerici*, which can refer as in RB itself to lesser ministers who could not celebrate Mass. One could therefore argue that Agde is referring to ministers such as *ostiarii* functioning like ushers at the dismissals, much as Cassian's monk envisioned himself *celebrare velut diaconum catechumenis missam.* The Agde text is thus not decisive in interpreting RB 60.4.

This does not rule out the possibility that an abbot might allow monastic presbyters to celebrate the eucharist in his monastery, although this by no means goes without saying.[58] But this is not what RB 60.4 is really talking about. In a context of cautiously allowing *quis de ordine sacerdotum* to be monks in a lay community, RB is concerned that the often large sense of "persona" such ministers no doubt had should be kept in bounds by the full discipline of the Rule, which must apply to all. Whatever honor is conceded to ordained monastics RB keeps in bounds by associating it strictly with the abbot's own unordained liturgical function within the monastery. In these liturgical functions, precisely, the ordained monastic may be allowed to take his place along with the abbot and outside the normal rank of seniority, to which he thereafter returns. He may also, in these functions only, *benedicere aut* (= *et*) *missas tenere*, acts which the context suggests the abbot himself regularly did.

The one thing, however, which no unordained abbot could do was to preside at a eucharistic celebration. But as spiritual master of the community there was a solid precedent for him to preside—like AT's catechist and the bishop in Laodicea, AC, Egeria, and elsewhere—at the office dismissals in his own oratory. Indeed, liturgical protocol of the period would have required that monks not leave an oratory office without first being formally dismissed by the abbot. This dismissal seems to have followed the precedent we have already seen for liturgical *missae:* petitionary prayer and hand laying, rendered in RB 60.4 as *benedicere aut missas tenere.* After the prayer, the monks came to the abbot's hand in order of seniority as they left the oratory. There is no reason to think that the abbot may not have associated an ordained monastic with himself at this perhaps burdensome task, or that he may not have allowed one of them to substitute for him in performing the dismissals in his absence. The abbot's doing such a thing would have been a prudent pastoral gesture to ordained monastics for maintaining harmony in the community. But RB is clear that this is something which belongs to the abbot alone by right, and to the ordained monastic only by abbatial concession: *si tamen iusserit ei abbas.* In view of this a more satisfactory translation of RB 60.4 might be: "[The ordained monastic] may, however, be conceded rank with the abbot when it comes to saying the blessing prayer and performing the dismissals [by hand laying], provided the abbot bids him do so."

This allows one to perceive better how communion may have been administered by the abbot or his substitute after sext or none before the common meal. After the concluding litany a prayer would have been said by the abbot, the kiss of peace exchanged, and then the community in rank of seniority came to his hand as usual, in this case to be communicated by him from the reserved sacrament before leaving the oratory for the refectory and the common meal. The phrase *post missas* in this instance is synecdoche for the office which ends formally in a communion service based on the dismissal ceremony common to all the day offices and compline.

Although this reconstruction cannot be absolutely certain given the nature of the evidence, it is plausible and would fit easily into the structural analysis we have been pursuing. It would also illustrate once again the versatility of *missa* structure, this time in a monastic office context generally, and in a communion context specifically, during the early sixth century.

As the *missa* structure appears to wane in public usage during the following centuries, to what extent it survived in monasteries cannot clearly be determined. But the spreading synecdoche of *missa* for the entire eucharistic celebration, rather than for certain specific parts of it, no doubt affected monastic sentiment as it did everyone else's. This would be particularly so as regards the old practice of monastic communion, pressing it to give way to more frequent celebration of Mass by the growing numbers of the *ordo sacerdotum* in monasteries. In such a changed atmosphere it would be difficult not to construe *post missas et communionem* of RB 38.2, and *missas tenere* of 60.4, as references to eucharistic celebration. But there is one other permutation in the history of *missa* usage which needs mention, namely, the dismissals which were used at communion time and survive as the "prayers of inclination."

5. DISMISSALS BEFORE COMMUNION: PRAYERS OF INCLINATION [59]
We have seen that the original purpose of the *missa* structure of prayer and hand laying appears from AT

18–19 and Egeria to have been formally to seal and terminate a specific unit of public instruction or worship. After such a conclusion the assembly of worshipers dispersed into the other activities of daily life or, as Egeria makes clear, redeployed itself into another synaxis which followed closely on the first. During the fourth century, as the originally tightly-knit and smaller communities of Christians increased rapidly in size under imperial favor, to become looser assemblies with growing numbers of functionally permanent catechumens and back-sliding baptized, large numbers of perennial non-communicants became standard. Not only did catechumenal and penitential policy become stricter, but eucharistic policy increasingly emphasized the awesomeness of this sacrament, the need for receiving it worthily, and the expectation that those able to receive it do so. As Taft observes, "The decline in frequent communion and the widespread practice of deferring baptism only contributed further to splitting the community into a communicating elite and the mass of catechumens, penitents, and others who were dismissed before the eucharist."[60]

That such a division of the community represented a growing pastoral problem which had immediate liturgical ramifications can be seen in contemporary sermons of church Fathers such as Cyril of Jerusalem, Theodore of Mopsuestia, and John Chrysostom, who complains "In vain is the daily sacrifice, in vain do we stand before the altar: no one partakes,"[61] much as we have already seen Caesarius of Arles doing in Gaul a century later. Obviously indifference or hyperphobia before the awesomeness of the mysteries was putting people off from going to communion and thus turning the Church's behavior on the Lord's Day into a form of personal devotion for the unusually pious. As a result a dismissal was added to the eucharist along with the old dismissals after the Word service, namely, a dismissal of non-communicants just prior to communion.

Taft notes that this made a virtue out of necessity, given the large numbers of non-communicants who were now remaining even after catechumens, penitents, and others had been dismissed at the end of the eucharistic Word service. Communion was often a rowdy affair, described by Chrysostom as filled with kicking, striking, anger, shoving, and disorder.[62] This behavior was made worse by non-communicants leaving on the brink of communion. It was to tidy this up, Taft thinks, that a *missa* of remaining non-communicants was introduced in the late fourth or early fifth century just before the invitation to communion. It involved a litany (*aiteseis*) followed by a collect known as the "Prayer of Inclination" because those being dismissed bowed their heads to receive the "blessing" of this prayer by the bishop, who frequently said it as he extended his hands over the whole group. This gesture would have avoided adding to the tumult at communion time that would have been occasioned by having the dismissed come individually to the bishop's hand. Taft translates the Byzantine prayer as follows:

"We give you thanks, O invisible king, who in your infinite power fashioned all things, and in the abundance of your mercy bring everything from nonexistence into being. Look down. . .on those who have bowed down their heads to you. . .Therefore, O Master, smooth out for all of us, for [our own] good, according to each one's need, whatever lies before us: sail with the seafarers, journey with the wayfarers, heal the sick, O physician of our souls and bodies. By the grace and mercies of your only-begotten Son. . ."[63]

The diaconal litany preceding this prayer petitions similarly, in particular "For an angel of peace, a faithful guide, a guardian of our souls and bodies," evoking a rich set of biblical images touching the ordinary concerns of daily life into which the non-communicants are being dismissed.[64] The translations of this prayer, found in all Eastern liturgies except the East Syrian, paradoxically make it a communion preparation prayer by rendering *ta prokeimena. . .eksomalison* (Taft's "smooth out for all of us. . .whatever lies before us") as "administer these offerings to all of us," or some such. But Taft shows convincingly that *ta prokeimena* does not refer to the gifts but, due to the verb *eksomalison*, to those things which lie before the dismissed in the daily life to which they are now returning, rather as does the Byzantine dismissal prayer at vespers.[65] The imagery is of God's presence and angelic help to wayfarers on the road of daily life as they reenter it on leaving the eucharist at which they do not partake.

The same pastoral and liturgical problem of non-communicants existed in Gaul in the sixth century. Caesarius of Arles preached against people leaving at the end of the eucharistic Word service so that hardly anyone was left to complete the mysteries, as we have seen. Under Caesarius the Council of Agde (506) forbade anyone to leave before the "blessing" of the bishop,[66] something which was neither the dismissal prayer for catechumens or penitents, nor the final "blessing" at the end of Mass, but a "prayer of inclination" done at a dismissal of non-communicants before communion in Gallican usage. In six parts, punctuated by Amens from the assembly, this prayer concluded with a deacon announcing: *Si quis non communicat det locum.*[67]

A similar arrangement may underlie a North African statement from the beginning of the fifth century in canon 12 of the Council of Milevis: "And this also was resolved, that prayers or orations, or *missae* which have been approved of in council, whether *praefationes* or *commendationes* or *manus impositiones*, shall be used by all."[68] Augustine complains of the length of time it took him to dismiss penitents, perhaps still individually coming to his hand, as we have seen. In North Africa not only were catechumens dismissed with prayer and episcopal hand laying at the end of the eucharistic Word service, but penitents and other non-communicants were dismissed similarly before communion.[69] Gregory the Great (+ 604) witnesses to what appears to be similar communion practice at Rome.[70]

6. SUMMARY

This chapter has attempted to assemble and analyze evidence of the presence, role, and extent of liturgical dismissals in early sources. It has pointed out that dismissals regularly consisted in prayer and some form of hand laying by the senior minister present (regularly the bishop) upon those individuals being dismissed. As numbers of those dismissed grew, it was noted, the hand laying with increasing frequency became an extension of hands over entire groups.

The dismissal structure, commonly referred to in Latin sources as *missa, impositio manuum,* or *benedictio,* occurred in a variety of circumstances: at the end of catechetical instructions, of offices in both cathedral and monastic settings, of the eucharistic Word service for the non-baptized and penitents, and of the eucharist proper for all the faithful; before communion for non-communicants; and apparently as the structural form by which penitents were reconciled and monks were communicated from the reserved sacrament by their abbot or an ordained monastic to whom he could concede this honor. The dismissal structure was highly versatile, being used in one context or another to affect every group within the liturgical assembly— catechumens, penitents, the illuminated, energumens, monastic ascetics, non-communicants, and the faithful generally. Its form and use were legislated in church orders, synods, councils, and rubrics. It is mentioned and commented on by travelers, bishops, preachers, pastors, and historians of the times.

The dismissal was carried out somewhat differently in various churches in both East and West. But its use in them all was frequent and general, so much so that, by the time it began to dissipate and fall into disuse from the seventh to eighth centuries, *missa* had in the West become a synecdoche for offices and, especially, the eucharist as a whole.

It may be particularly noteworthy that in AT, our earliest source for the *missa*'s structure and use, the bishop himself, as the supreme catechist, followed the practice of prayer and hand laying, expanded in this solemn instance by an exsufflation and signation, to "exorcize" the catechumens at their final meeting before their baptism. It appears to be the last catechetical act for them before he will similarly pray and lay his hand on them with an anointing and signation *after* their baptism, as we shall see.

NOTES

1. Aidan Kavanagh, "Confirmation: A Suggestion from Structure." *Worship* 58 (1984) 386–395.

2. It has been suggested, for example, that the galleries in large churches such as Hagia Sophia in Constantinople, which exit by stairways opening directly to the *outside* of the church, were intended to facilitate the dismissals of catechumens so as not to disturb unduly the remaining faithful on the main level; T. Mathews, *The Early Churches of Constantinople: Architecture and Liturgy* (University Park, Pennsylvania 1971). But the evidence clearly notes, as we shall see, that those being dismissed leave the church only after coming to have the bishop's hands laid on them after prayer, something which may weaken Mathews's theory. That crowd con-

trol was indeed necessary in Hagia Sophia is suggested by the large numbers of *ostiarii* attached to it, which Justinian *limited* to one hundred.

3. See Robert Taft, *The Great Entrance* (Rome 1975) 84–85, 213–214.

4. G. J. Cuming, *Hippolytus: A Text for Students* (Bramcote, Notts. 1976) 16–17; G. Dix, *The Apostolic Tradition of St. Hippolytus of Rome* [1937] (London ²1968) 29–30; B. Botte, *La Tradition Apostolique de saint Hippolyte* (Münster 1963) 40. The English of AT is from Cuming throughout, the Latin from Botte.

5. Section 41 in Cuming 29; Botte 88; Dix 61–62.

6. Section 17 in Cuming 16; Botte 38; Dix 28.

7. Sections 20–21 in Cuming 17–18 and Botte 42–44; Dix 32–33.

8. In AT there are some fifteen references to hand laying. Six of these specify where it is *not* to occur. Four have epicleses of the Holy Spirit as their prayer. Only four references are to baptism and none of these are epicleses, at least in the earliest surviving text of AT, the Latin translation known as the Verona palimpsest, as we shall see.

9. See T. Talley, *The Origins of the Liturgical Year* (New York 1986) 200.

10. See J. Heinemann, *Prayer in the Talmud: Forms and Patterns* (Berlin and New York 1977); T. Talley, "From *Berakah* to *Eucharistia*: A Reopening Question." *Worship* 50 (1976) 115–137, and "The Literary Structure of the Eucharistic Prayer," *Worship* 58 (1984) 404–420.

11. Touched on by Taft, *The Great Entrance* 370–372.

12. Mansi 2.567; English in Schaff-Wace 14.136.

13. This same tripartite bidding form is, of course, still evident in the Roman solemn intercessions on Good Friday.

14. Cuming 16; Dix 29; Botte 40.

15. Cuming 17; Dix 31; Botte 42.

16. Cuming 24–25; Dix 45–46; Botte 68.

17. A review of the dating is in *Liturgies Eastern and Western*, F.E. Brightman, ed. (Oxford 1896) xxviii–xxix.

18. Brightman 3–27 (Greek). English translation is in *The Liturgy of the Eighth Book of "The Apostolic Constitutions"commonly called the Clementine Liturgy*, R. H. Cresswell, trans. and ed. (London ²1924). The standard study and edition is F.X. Funk, *Didascalia et Constitutiones Apostolorum* (Paderborn 1905).

19. The prayers for the energumens point to who these people were: those whom Jesus himself was at pains to aid, people whose inexplicable behavior put them beyond conventional society. They appear to be those who did not suffer from conventionally diagnosed diseases, but from psychic disorders such as epilepsy, severe "ticks," and psychotic manias resulting in seemingly random alterations in behavior causing social astonishment and alarm. See F.J. Dölger. *Antike und Christentum* vol. 1 (Münster 1934) 95–137.

20. Cresswell 40, note 2.

21. For text and commentary see J. Wilkinson. *Egeria's Travels* (London 1971); revised edition, *Egeria's Travels to the Holy Land* (Jerusalem 1981). Also *Itinerarium Egeriae. Editio critica*, A. Franceschini and R. Weber (CCL 175, Brepols-Turnholt 1958). Paragraph references from Wilkinson.

22. J.A. Jungmann, *The Mass of the Roman Rite* (New York 1951) 1.333–336, dates use of the *kyrie eleison* in Rome and the West to the fifth century and later.

23. See C. Mohrmann, "Missa," *Vigiliae Christianae* 12 (1958) 67–92.

24. Mohrmann, 80; see also K. Gamber, *Missa Romensis* (Regensburg 1972) 170–186.

25. Wilkinson 57 thinks "presumably to kiss it." But in view of AT 19, Laodicea 19, and probably AC 8 it would be better to construe the phrase as referring to a hand laying on the

individual by the bishop. That the dismissed may then have kissed the bishop's hand is not improbable, but it would not have been the fundamental gesture.

26. The sort of evidence Egeria gives allows us to see through her eyes not only how a major early liturgy was celebrated, but even how the churches were decorated in Jerusalem and Bethlehem for the Epiphany (25.8–10). This is the sort of evidence we rarely get until much later.

27. Mohrmann 78 notes that the Latin word *missa*, from *dimissio*, is extremely rare outside liturgical usage. See F.J. Dölger, *Antike und Christentum* vol. 4 (Münster 1934) 271–275.

28. Epistle 149.6 (CSEL 44.363); Sermon 232.7–8 (PL 38.1111). In North Africa, as we shall see, the dismissal of penitents seems to have occurred just before communion.

29. Sozomen, *Hist. Eccl.* 7.16 (PG67.1459). See James Dallen, *The Reconciling Community: The Rite of Penance* (New York 1986) 68.

30. See Dallen 69–73.

31. On the episcopal dismissal of penitents as the "blessing of penance" see 3 Arles 24 (Mansi 9.18) and *Vita Hilarii* 13, 16 (PL 50.1233). Also J.A. Jungmann, *Die lateinischen Bussriten in ihrer geschichtlichen Entwicklung* (Innsbruck 1932) 35–38; Dallen 67–68.

32. Thus Mohrmann 83, following L. Duchesne, *Origines du Culte chrétiene* [1899] (Paris 1925) 512.

33. Wilkinson 58. Liturgical synecdoche such as this goes back to the beginning of Christian tradition. The verb *eucharistein*, "to give thanks," becomes a noun referring to the form of prayer, to the whole service, and to the bread and wine involved in it. See *Didache* 9.1 and 5; Ignatius *Ephesians* 13.1, *Smyrnians* 7.1, *Philadelphians* 4; Justin *Dialogue* 41.1 and 3, 70.4; *1 Apology* 66.1 and 2; AT 21 (Botte 54). See R. Kaczynski, "The Lima Text in the Light of Historical Research," *Studia Liturgica* 16 (1986) 22–39, especially 28.

34. Epistle 20.4f. (PL 16.995); Mohrmann 85–86.

35. See Mohrmann 87–89.

36. Sermon 73, quoted in Mohrmann 88.

37. Jungmann, *The Mass of the Roman Rite* 1.478, note 24.

38. See P. Borella, "La 'missa' o 'dimissio catechumenorum' nelle liturgia occidentali," *Ephemerides Liturgicae* 53 (1939) 60–110.

39. Jungmann 479.

40. For the text see Jungmann 336–337.

41. Jungmann 482, note 15.

42. Brightman 9–13.

43. *Exposit. in Psalm.* 25 and 33; Mohrmann 89.

44. J.A. Jungmann, *Gewordene Liturgie* (Innsbruck 1941) 41.

45. *The Rule of the Master*, L. Eberle and C. Phipps eds. (Kalamazoo 1977); *RB 1980: The Rule of St. Benedict*, T. Fry et al. eds. (Collegeville, Minnesota 1980).

46. Thus J. McCann, *The Rule of St. Benedict* (London 1952) 61. In RB 12.4 and 13.11 *et completum est* is used in this sense, but not *missa*.

47. This later image of prayers *transmissae ad Deum* goes back to Hildebert of LeMans' early twelfth century explanation of the Mass (Pl 171.1172). See B. Linderbauer, *S. Benedicti Regula Monachorum* (Metten 1922) 254; Mohrmann 69 and 81.

48. Thus Mohrmann 82. This is in sharp distinction from the office use of *missa* in Southern Gaul and Spain, where the term refers to a unit of psalms, canticles, and sometimes readings; Jordi Pinell, "El oficio hispano-visigotico," *Hispania Sacra* 10 (1957) 404; Robert Taft, *The Liturgy of the Hours in East and West* (Collegeville 1986) 116, 147–149.

49. A. deVogüé, "Problems of the Monastic Conventual Mass," *The Downside Review* 87 (1969) 328. There was daily communion but not Mass in Egyptian monasteries in the

late fourth century; see R. Taft, *Beyond East and West: Problems in Liturgical Understanding* (Washington 1984) 69.

50. See *RB 1980* 411–412; E. de Bhaldraithe, "Problems of the Monastic Conventual Mass," *The Downside Review* 90 (1972) 170.

51. *RB 1980* 271, 273 so translates the text.

52. DeVogüé 327 accepts it as eucharistic; B. Steidle, *The Rule of St. Benedict* (Canon City, Colorado 1967) 260–262 does not.

53. As Taft, *Beyond East and West* 68–69, observes, the monastic problem was ". . .how to keep the monks separated from the laity, and at the same time protect them from the pride, ambition, envy, and challenge to the lay-abbot's authority that could ensue from introducing priests into the ranks."

54 RB 60.8, 61.12, 65.3.

55. *RB 1980* 273. The corresponding passage in RM 83.5 mentions prayers and blessings but not *missas*.

56. B. Steidle, "Commentationes in Regulam S. Benedicti," *Studia Anselmiana* 42 (1957) 100f.

57. Mohrmann 89.

58. See note 53. In contemporary Gaul it seems that monks and nuns did not leave their enclosures for Mass even on Sundays, but received communion from the presanctified after terce. Robert Taft, *The Liturgy of the Hours in East and West* (Collegeville 1986) 107. This may be what RB 38.2 has in mind; see p. 23, above.

59. See R. Taft, "The Inclination Prayer before Communion in the Byzantine Liturgy of St. John Chrysostom: A Study in Comparative Liturgy," *Ecclesia Orans* 3:1 (1986) 29–60.

60. Taft 43.

61. *In Eph. hom.* 3,4 (PG 62.28); see Taft 44.

62. *De baptismo Christi* 4 (PG 49.370); see Taft 47.

63. Taft 31–32.

64. Isaiah 40.3–5, cited in the opening of the gospels (Matthew 3.3, Mark 1.2–3, Luke 3.4–5, John 1.23). Taft 46–47 notes the "angel of peace" allusion in Basil's Letter 11, and in Chrysostom's commentary on the Antiochene litany for dismissing catechumens in his *In 2 Cor. hom.* 2.2 (PG 61. 403–404); Taft 35.

65. Taft 32–37. An analogous dismissal prayer before communion is in the euchologion of the fourth century bishop Serapion of Egypt; see Taft 38.

66. Canon 47; Mansi 8. 332. Also in canon 22 (26) of Orleans I (511) and canon 29 of Orleans III (538); Mansi 8. 355 and 9.19. Taft 49.

67. See K. Gamber, *Ordo antiquus Gallicanus. Der gallikanische Messeritus des 6. Jahrhunderts* (Regensburg 1965) 40–41; Taft 50. Gregory the Great at Rome reports the same words by the deacon in his *Dialogues* 2:23.4 (SC 260.206–208).

68. CCL 149, 365; E. Kilmartin, "Early African Legislation concerning Liturgical Prayer," *Ephemerides Liturgicae* 99 (1985) 110–111; Taft 51.

69 Taft 51–54.

70. See note 67.

Chapter Two

A Baptismal *Missa*

Evidence concerning the place, structure, and purpose
of dismissal rites is relatively abundant in liturgical literature from the early third through the sixth centuries. The purpose of the *missa* rite was to conclude and
formally "seal" a unit of public worship or instruction
by dismissing the assembly either in whole or part
with prayer and by physical contact between the dismissed and its chief minister—bishop, catechist, abbot
or, by concession, ordained monastic.

The *missa* took place at the end of a distinct unit of
liturgical prayer, lections, psalmody, and instruction
(such as an office or the eucharistic service of the
Word), or of sacramental worship (such as the eucharistic banquet from the prayers of the faithful through
the communion or, as we shall see, the initiatory unit
of baptism and its chrismation). The *missa* of one liturgical unit often occurred even though another liturgical unit was to begin immediately, almost as preparation for it—as when catechumens and others were
dismissed at the end of the Word service before the
eucharistic banquet began with the prayers of the faithful, or when non-communicants were dismissed just
before communion.

As the number of variously motivated worshipers increased after the legitimization of Christianity in the
early fourth century the *missa* rite also grew in complexity and length. It came to involve not only bishops

at large public services but also deacons, *ostiarii* and other clerics whose purpose was not leading in prayer but crowd control. In monasteries the rite of communion from the reserved sacrament at the abbot's hand appears to have been intimately related to the *missa* rite. So prominent a feature did the rite become that it began to lend its name to the whole liturgical unit it concluded, namely, to offices and, from the fifth century onward, to the eucharist in the West.

The *missa* rite's structure remained fundamentally bipartite. First, there was petitionary prayer by the presiding minister, often with diaconal assistance, in bidding or litanic and collect forms. Second, this was followed by each of the dismissed coming under the presiding minister's hand, probably by class, rank, or seniority. As numbers increased, this bipartite rite began to be performed by presidential prayer said with hands extended over the whole group (the *oratio super populum* retained in the Roman liturgy during Lent)[1] as they responded with bowed heads and then dispersed without any longer coming individually to be touched by the presiding minister. Later, even the extension of hands over the whole group would be reduced to a sign of the cross, and the collect prayer to a short blessing formula. Abuses crept in: persons not yet dismissed left with those who were being dismissed after the sermon at the end of the eucharistic Word service. Dismissals at this point in the liturgy began to disappear in practice even though the rite remained in liturgical books and commentaries. For a while, at least, the dismissal of non-communicants took place just before communion in some places. Only the dismissal of all at the end of the eucharist finally survived, but in the diminished form mentioned above.

This is what became of the euchology and logistics of a rite known from Egeria to RB and after as *missa*. It is thus not surprising that modern commentators are often unable to detect *missa* structures in early liturgies, much less to account for them or interpret them in their original contexts. That this inability may have affected our grasp of the origins of confirmation I have already suggested.[2] In view of the evidence concerning liturgical dismissals summarized in Chapter One it may now be possible to direct that evidence toward confirmation's origins.

1. THE APOSTOLIC TRADITION

The earliest account of a structure which we today recognize as confirmation occurs in AT 21.[3] About this rite, which follows baptism and an anointing with consecrated oil by a presbyter, the literature is extensive and contentious. Dix says that as AT's rite of baptism is derived from the Jewish baptismal rite for proselytes, so AT's rite of confirmation plays the same role which circumcision, "the seal of the covenant," plays in the initiation of a gentile convert to Judaism.[4] This view, however, presumes dependency of Christian baptism on proselyte baptism, which is dubious,[5] and appears to give a more important role to AT's signing on the forehead than does AT itself. Dix heads this section of AT "confirmation," a term nowhere in the text. He calls this rite "the sealing" although, again, no such terminology is in the text beyond the stipulation that one *signs* or is *signed* (*consignans, signatus est*) on the forehead during the hand laying. For Dix all "seals" become confirmation, even when they occur prior to baptism, as in East Syria.[6] Scholars then search for confirmation in other early liturgies and patristic sources.[7] One writer, despite significant differences in New Testament allusions to baptismal practice,[8] finds confirmation intimated in Acts 8 and in the Lukan community's theology of the Holy Spirit.[9] Byzantines, Armenians, and Syrians discover that their postbaptismal chrismations are "confirmation," and Latin theologians find in confirmation a supplying of graces, an increase in baptismal grace, and a de-layed, even separate, gift or set of gifts of the Holy Spirit beyond baptism. The American Episcopal *Book of Common Prayer* in 1979 has at baptism only a postbaptismal signation with or without chrism, but leaves the hand laying as something bishops may do later, even repeatedly, for a variety of reasons. Confirmation today does seem to be a sacrament in search of its roots and meaning, and the search is filled with equivocation over what is being searched for.[10]

This state of affairs results at least in part from relying on theological interpretations and the history of doctrine to define the questions, and thus to determine the answers, rather than on an analysis of the liturgical structures of confirmation for which we have some hard evidence. This evidence begins in AT 21, where the *structure* may first be discerned. Accounting for this evidence may make it possible to see the structural origin of confirmation in a wider context already adumbrated in Chapter One. Discerning this wider context may shed some light on what it is we are talking about, and bring into sharper focus the implications of what was at stake when the structure and its contents were repeatedly reinterpreted in later centuries. In what follows, therefore, our primary purpose is not to reconcile later theological interpretations of confirmation with its origins, much less to depend upon the history of doctrine to reveal those origins. It is instead to pursue the structural analyst's question of *what* it is that gets interpreted later in a discourse of the second order.[11] What, then, is the structure of the rite which comes between baptism and the eucharist in AT 21?

An answer to this question should begin with two preliminary admonitions. First, one must recall how baptism ends in AT 21. The rite of baptism is extensive,[12] beginning with prayer over the water at cockcrow and episcopal thanksgiving over, and exorcism of, two oils. After each person has been baptized, ". . .when he has come up. . .he shall be anointed from the oil which was sanctified [by the thanksgiving prayer of the bishop] by the presbyter, who says: I anoint you with holy oil in the name of Jesus Christ. And so each of them shall wipe themselves and put on their clothes, and then they shall enter into the church [*et postea in ecclesia ingrediantur*]."[13] This last phrase may indicate that from this time forward the newly baptized and anointed are regarded as Church members. But in view of what follows this abstract meaning is unlikely. More probably the phrase refers to the now anointed and dressed neophytes leaving the place of baptism and going in to where the *ecclesia*, the assembly, is publicly gathered. It is there, not in the place of baptism, that what follows will be done.

What AT 21 is talking about is probably not a move from one building (the baptistery) to another (the church), but a move from one place to another within a single building such as the house-church at Dura Europas dating from this same period; that is, from a baptismal room,[14] discreetly enclosed due to the nudity of the baptismal candidates, to a perhaps larger and more open room where the *ecclesia* was assembled at prayer during the baptisms. The setting seems to be a *domus ecclesiae*, a "house of the assembly;" the move takes place only after the neophytes are fully dressed so as to be publicly presentable.

It is in the midst of this assembly then that the bishop (who seems to have done nothing so far but bless the oils and preside) says and does certain things with regard to the neophytes which would, within such a setting, have been sensed by all present as the public conclusion of something which had begun more privately *in camera*. These things having been done, concluding not only the baptismal service but the

43

assembly's time of prayer, the newly enlarged *ecclesia* would then have had to redeploy itself in order to proceed with the Oblation, as AT calls the eucharist, beginning with the prayers of the faithful (*cum omni populo orent*), the kiss of peace (*de ore pacem offerant*), and the presentation of bread and wine by deacons to the bishop for him to give thanks over (*tunc iam offeratur oblatio a diaconibus episcopo et gratias agat*).[15]

The second admonition is that we should remember the occurrence of what we have identified as a *missa* rite in the dismissal of catechumens by their catechist with prayer and hand laying in AT 19.[16] Keeping this precedent from within the same document in mind, together with what we saw in Chapter One of the development of such a structure later, we may now examine what the bishop says and does in regard to the neophytes as they take their places in the assembly for the first time, after their baptism and anointing by a presbyter "with holy oil in the name of Jesus Christ."[17]

AT 21 says what the bishop does first: *Episcopus uero manu(m) illis inponens inuocet dicens . . .*[18] What this involves is stipulated in the sequence of the text which follows. The bishop first says a petitionary prayer in the plural number for all the newly baptized. It is a collect for the neophytes, what Egeria will call a "Prayer for All":

"Lord God, you have made them worthy to receive remission of sins through the laver of regeneration of the Holy Spirit;

"send upon them your grace, that they may serve you according to your will; for to you is glory, to Father and Son with the Holy Spirit in the holy Church, both now and to the ages of ages. Amen."[19]

Then, pouring from his hand the same oil that was used for the postbaptismal anointing by the presbyter onto the neophyte's head, and laying his hand on the head, the bishop says:

"I anoint you with holy oil in God the Father almighty and Christ Jesus and the holy Spirit."[20]

The bishop, perhaps with his thumb as his hand still lies on the neophyte's head, then signs (*consignans*) the forehead, surely in the sign of the cross, either saying nothing or doing the signing while saying the anointing declaration quoted above. Bishop and neophyte then exchange for the first time the Christian kiss, saying as they do so *Dominus tecum: Et cum spiritu tuo*. The text concludes: "So let him do with each one. And then they shall pray together with all the people: they do not pray with the faithful until they have carried out these things. And when they have prayed, they shall give the kiss of peace."[21]

This four-step procedure of 1) episcopal prayer over all, followed by 2) an individual hand laying with 3) anointing and signation, and 4) kiss and greeting is what AT 21 means when it says *Episcopus uero manu(m) illis inponens inocet dicens*. Since *manum* is accusative singular due to *inponens* ("The bishop placing a hand on them"), this rules out a general extension of both hands over the whole group; nor does it seem logical that he would place a hand on each single neophyte while repeatedly reciting a petitionary prayer using pronouns in the plural number. The text does not say *extendens* but *inponens*, implying physical touch, as when it says of the anointing: *Postea oleum sanctificatum infunde(n)s de manu et inponens in capite.*[22]

What AT 21 says the bishop is to do is the following:

1. Say a prayer for all the neophytes (*inuocet dicens. . .*);

2. Lay his hand, holding oil in the palm, on each of the neophytes' heads (*manum illis inponens. . .*),

3. Signing each on the forehead with his thumb (*consignans in frontem. . .*),

4. And ending by greeting each with words and a kiss (*offerat osculum et dicat. . .*).

This is the sequence which the text describes, with the necessary shift in grammatical number from plural in the petitionary "Lord God" prayer to singular as each neophyte comes under the bishop's hand.[23]

The fundamental structure of this postbaptismal rite performed by the bishop is one of prayer and of coming under the bishop's hand at the end of one liturgical unit (baptism and its presbyteral anointing) before continuing on to another liturgical unit (the baptismal eucharist, about which AT 21 makes several special dispositions).[24] AT's four-step sequence appears to be a carefully described instance of what we have already seen will be called in later sources a *missa*, and it functions in the same way in this particularly solemn instance. Even though AT does not assign any specific baptismal duties to the bishop except for his giving thanks over one oil and exorcizing the other,[25] he nonetheless does the *missa*, as Egeria notes of the bishop in connection even with an office from which he is absent, as we have seen.

In addition to the underlying structure of prayer and hand laying in AT 21, another matter may suggest *missa* procedure here. No surviving *missa* prayer takes the form of an epiclesis of the Holy Spirit. Given where in the liturgy such prayers were said (at dismissals), and over whom they were said (catechumens, penitents, the whole assembly), there would have been no motive for invoking the Holy Spirit in such contexts: the substantive liturgical business was either to come (e.g., in the eucharist proper) or already over (e.g., the eucharist, baptism, etc.). In the case of catechumens and penitents moreover, there would be no question of invoking the Holy Spirit upon the non-baptized or those under penance. It is not surprising, then, that the bishop's "Lord God" prayer in the Verona *Urtext* of AT 21 is *not* an epiclesis of the Holy Spirit. What the prayer asks for is not the descent of the Holy Spirit but that God might send grace upon the neophytes, who have already undergone the *lauacrum regenerationis spiritus sancti*, "that they may serve you according to your will." The usual explanation for this apparent omission of the Holy Spirit in a prayer of "confirmation" is that, in view of later translations of the document which do construe the prayer as an epiclesis, the Verona text is corrupt.[26] Yet as Lampe has pointed out, the Latin grammar shows no signs of corruption and can be translated as it stands.[27]

While it is true that translations of AT in other languages such as Arabic and Ethiopic render the "Lord God" prayer as an epiclesis of the Holy Spirit, these texts are very much later than the Verona Latin version, which was done c. 350; the Arabic and Ethiopic versions date from the thirteenth century, over nine centuries later.[28] The probability is strong that these later translations represent a development of AT on this matter which was unknown when the document was written and the Verona translation was made.

The text of the "Lord God" prayer in the Verona translation clearly associates the Holy Spirit with *baptism*, the "bath of regeneration of the Holy Spirit," in complete harmony with Titus 3.5 and John 3.5. AT is not alone in this. Later Western baptismal allusions make similar associations. Ambrose in the late fourth century quotes the formula in Milan for the postbaptismal anointing with *myron:* "God the Father Almighty . . . who has regenerated you by water and the Holy Spirit, and has forgiven you your sins, himself anoints you for eternal life."[29] The same phraseology occurs in postbaptismal chrismations in the *Gelasian*

Sacramentary, reflecting Roman usage by the eighth century,[30] in the *Missale Gallicanum Vetus,* and the *Bobbio Missal.*[31] The burden of these texts, as is typical of postbaptismal chrismations, is not pneumatic and the formulaic references to baptismal regeneration by water and Holy Spirit for the remission of sins point more to a messianic function referred to in Titus 3.5, John 3.5, and 1 Corinthians 12.13 than to an alleged Lukan pneumatology in Acts 8.

Whatever else may be said about Lukan pneumatology, it is not reflected in AT 21 unless one is prepared to rewrite the "Lord God" prayer as given in the Verona translation according to the conjectures of Dix and Botte. The Verona version of this prayer is clearly in conformity with a messianic theme in New Testament literature and early Latin liturgical sources. It suggests moreover that the fundamental business of baptism, the *lauacrum regenerationis spiritus sancti,* is accomplished by water and a messianic-christic anointing before the baptismal action is structurally consummated in a dismissal made up of prayer ("Lord God") and hand laying on the neophytes by the bishop. That this prayer and hand laying add something new to baptism is a perception based on subsequent alterations to the "Lord God" text.[32] In Verona terms, at least, what the "Lord God" prayer and hand laying could add to the messianic gift of regeneration by water and the Holy Spirit in baptism for the forgiveness of sins is theologically difficult to imagine. That the "something new" is the Holy Spirit itself is simply not in the Verona text of AT 21 and would be sacramentally tautological if it were. To argue otherwise is anachronistic and symptomatic of failure to apprehend the *missa* structure which the "Lord God" prayer and the hand laying by the bishop comprise. To this matter we shall have to return later.

Meanwhile, it should be noted that even though an epiclesis of the Holy Spirit does not occur in the postbaptismal *missa* of AT 21 such an epiclesis does occur in the type of eucharistic prayer cited in AT 4 as a model, at least, of how a newly ordained bishop is to pray at the Oblation.[33] The epicletic section of this eucharistic prayer follows directly after the anamnesis and oblation:

"And we ask that you would send your Holy Spirit upon the offering of your holy Church;

"that, gathering (it) into one, you would grant to all who partake of the holy things (to partake) for the fullness of the Holy Spirit for the strengthening [*ad confirmationem*] of faith in truth, that we may praise and glorify you through your child Jesus Christ . . ."[34]

The neophytes very probably would have heard this or something like it during their baptismal eucharist, which AT 21 describes in detail following the section on the *missa*.[35] Thus in the structural scenario of AT's initiation liturgy as a whole the Holy Spirit acts in the *lauacrum regenerationis* and is formally asked for in its fullness for the strengthening of the whole community's "faith in truth" in the eucharist. The *missa*, which marks off the baptismal from the eucharistic phases of initiation, prays only for God's grace so that the neophytes might serve God according to his will, a sentiment that is alluded to also in the anamnesis of the eucharistic prayer:

"Remembering therefore his death and resurrection, we offer to you the bread and cup, giving you thanks because you have held us worthy to stand before you and minister to you."[36]

"To serve you according to your will" in the *missa* "Lord God" prayer, and "to stand before you and minister to you" in the eucharistic prayer, together point to the kind of fundamental Christian service into which all Christians are baptized and anointed. It is not merely service to God's will in general as expressed in natural, religious, or civil law, but particular service which is consummated primarily in the priestly and messianic service of God (*hierateuein soi*) made possible by the Anointed One whose first gift is his own life-giving Spirit. The most immediate calling of the baptized is to divine service at the Holy Table in Christ, where they are strengthened in faith by the fullness of the Holy Spirit they receive there. All other Christian service, it may be inferred, flows from here.

It is significant that the only other prayers which invoke the Holy Spirit in the earliest form of AT occur in the ordinations of bishops, presbyters, and deacons and are replete with the language of ministry.[37] These orders of ministry undergo hand laying and have the Spirit invoked upon them; the newly baptized undergo a hand laying of dismissal and, with all the faithful, have the Spirit invoked upon them as they partake in the eucharist "for the strengthening [*ad confirmationem*] of faith in truth" that they may praise and glorify God in that service of ministry. Hieratic or priestly service to God by the Spirit given by the Messiah is thus generic among the baptized. What we today might call that ministry's executive functions are specific to bishops, presbyters, and deacons, who need hand laying and epicletic prayer on entry into their order of service. What happens in AT's baptismal *missa* is thus in no sense an "ordination." Rather, it releases the washed, forgiven, and anointed into the priestly, because messianic, ministry of the whole Church to God's will, consummated in the fullness of the Holy Spirit for the strengthening of the faith in truth at the eucharistic Oblation in an assembly "where the Holy Spirit flourishes" (AT 41).[38]

Burton Scott Easton was accurate when he observed in 1934: "Hippolytus contributes little to clarifying the difficult subject of Confirmation."[39] This is true for the most obvious of reasons: confirmation is not there. The bishop does not invoke the Holy Spirit on the neophytes in the "Lord God" prayer; nor is there any suggestion that laying his hand on them as he signs them on the forehead with oil, with the words "I anoint you with holy oil in God the Father almighty and Christ Jesus and the Holy Spirit," is to be construed as a special giving of the Holy Spirit.[40]

What the Verona text of AT 21 describes at this point is a bishop performing nothing more nor less than a *missa*, his proper liturgy for the neophytes. He does this by offering a prayer for them which refers back to their *lauacrum regenerationis spiritus sancti*. They then come under his hand as he anoints them in memory of their baptismal unction in the name of Jesus the Christ and marks their foreheads using words that once again evoke the Trinitarian form of their baptismal confession as they are about to exercise that confession for the first time in the Oblation. This is how their baptism is publicly sealed, perfected, consummated—not by adding something to it which it lacked, but by introducing them, now fully equipped, into its exercise. The way this is done is by a standard *missa*, the prayer and hand laying of which are tailored to the events of baptism and anointing which the neophytes had just undergone *in camera*. It is all quite scriptural and liturgically coherent, even rather elegant.

This analysis reveals that the church of AT is in agreement with various specific traditions of its time. When these traditions refer to "baptism" they mean a water bath either preceded or followed by a messianic anointing. The whole liturgical unit comprises the remission of sins by the *lauacrum regenerationis spiritus sancti*, the Spirit being the first gift of the Anointed-Messiah-Christ. East Syrians and Armenians originally did this messianic anointing before baptism,[41] West Syrians and others after baptism. In both cases messianism and pneumaticism are originally in intimate coordination. As in the New Testament, the Christ sends the Spirit by whom, alone, Jesus is known to be the Christ. Thus Cyril of Jerusalem (c. 315–386) explains to the newly baptized their postbaptismal chrismation in Jordan terms:

"[Christ][42] also bathed himself in the river Jordan, and having imparted the fragrance of his Godhead to the waters he came up from them. And the Holy Spirit in substance rested upon him, like resting on like. In the same manner to you also, after you had come up from the pool . . . was given the unction, the emblem of that wherewith Christ was anointed; and this is the Holy Spirit . . ."[43]

The context is thoroughly Christic. By the time of the eighth century *Barberini Euchologion*, however, Byzantine usage has submerged this messianism, calling the postbaptismal chrismation without qualification "the seal of the gift of the Holy Spirit."[44] By Cyril's time, toward the end of the fourth century, a pneumatic emphasis has begun to develop, centering on the chrismation after baptism and coming full term in the *Barberini Euchologion* of the eighth. This Eastern development is a portent of what is about to happen in Rome concerning the old episcopal *missa* in AT 21.

2.   INNOCENT I, CONSIGNATION, CONFIRMATION
So far we have spoken of the baptismal *missa* in AT 21 without any defense of its representing early third-century Roman practice, even though this is the current opinion of scholars. The merits of this opinion, which are considerable, are not however of direct concern here. Whatever one holds concerning AT's provenance, subsequent Roman tradition undeniably betrays AT's influence in that church's baptismal usage.

We have already noted the eighth-century *Gelasian Sacramentary's* revision of the bishop's "Lord God" prayer at the *missa* in AT 21, and we will have occasion to return to it later. The perdurance of that prayer, even in a recast epiclesis form, is one mark of AT's influence in later Roman initiatory usage. Another mark, less often commented on, is the tenacity with which episcopal ministry cleaves to the ending of baptism whether in *missa* form, or later as "consignation" in Rome itself, and as "confirmation" in Western churches generally, even as episcopal presidency at all other liturgical services was becoming less common and presbyteral presidency more usual. A third mark of AT's influence is the very survival of its *missa* structure of prayer and hand laying in later Roman usage. This structure is unknown in the East and originally alien to Gallican churches in the West, which incorporate the Roman structure somewhat reluctantly and only with adaptations.

Cyprian and Tertullian in Carthage mention a hand laying with invocation of the Holy Spirit after the postbaptismal anointing, concluding with a signation, as does Augustine in Hippo, more vaguely, some two centuries later.[45] Augustine's mentor Ambrose in Milan speaks of a "spiritual seal" and a "perfecting," by which he seems to mean an invocation of the Holy Spirit and its gifts on the neophytes that takes place after the postbaptismal anointing and footwashing.[46] While tantalizing, all this evidence remains allusive because we have no surviving liturgical texts from these eras and areas to compare with AT 21. Allusive evidence, especially in reference to actual liturgical practice, must be used carefully lest unwarranted generalizations and anachronisms be generated. If, for example, one reads the letter of John the Deacon to Sennarius (c. 500) by itself one might conclude from its allusions that the Roman baptismal liturgy of the time included only water baptism, clothing in white garments, and communion.[47] Similarly, if one reads Gallican councils' allusions to bishops "confirming" by laying hands and praying for the Holy Spirit on some occasions one might be tempted to conclude that the old Roman *missa*, or consignation, or something liturgically analogous to them is being referred to. Neither conclusion would be accurate.

As late as the eighth century, when Gallican liturgies were already falling into disuse, Gallican liturgical books record no liturgical ceremonies concluding baptism other than a presbyteral chrismation,[48] clothing, and foot washing—elements which resemble Milanese usage reported by Ambrose. Fourth and fifth century councils in Spain and southern Gaul direct bishops to "perfect," "complete," or "confirm" baptisms done by presbyters or deacons as a matter of pastoral or juridical oversight rather than of regular sacramental ministry: there is no reference in Gallican or Spanish liturgical books to a distinct episcopal rite after baptism.[49] Episcopal oversight was regarded as necessary in extraordinary situations such as emergency baptisms (Council of Elvira 38, 77), the reconciliation of heretics (Council of Arles 9), episcopal unavailability in rural areas (Council of Riez 3), or when chrism had been unavailable or omitted after baptism (Council of Orange 2).[50] The bishop regularizes such situations by a hand laying, which is said to involve the Holy Spirit *only* in the case of heretics being reconciled to the Church and apparently without prayer of any kind: *manus ei tantum imponatur, ut accipiat Spiritum*.[51] Outside southern Gaul the term *confirmatio* is not used of any ceremony after baptism but, as in the epiclesis of the eucharistic prayer in AT 4, of the eucharist; communion is said to "confirm" or strengthen the newly baptized participants.[52]

Hispano-Gallican "confirmation" thus bears no relationship to the episcopal *missa* rite we have seen in AT 21, although some resonance with AT 4 is possible when the term is used in a eucharistic context. Closer similarities are evident between the old Roman *missa* in AT 21 and the postchrismational rites alluded to in North Africa and Milan, although differences are also obvious. Rome knows no footwashing as in Milan and Gaul, nor does it appear originally to know an invocation of the Holy Spirit on the newly baptized and chrismated, as Cyprian and Tertullian do.[53] When Ambrose mentions the "spiritual seal" he nowhere specifies hand laying or an anointing, only an "invocation of the priest" which lists the seven gifts of the Spirit from Isaiah 11.2f. But as he explains this it is redolent of a certain messianism: "God the Father has sealed you. Christ the Lord has confirmed [or strengthened] you and given the earnest of the Spirit in your heart as you have learned from the apostolic lesson [2 Corinthians 1.21f.]"[54]

For Ambrose the "spiritual seal" is tied to the postbaptismal anointing with *myron* which, when poured on the head of a wise man (the neophyte), denotes grace perfecting wisdom for perfect works; this, he says, "is called regeneration."[55] From these allusions it is impossible to say with certainty what the liturgy of Ambrose's "spiritual seal" might actually have been, beyond a prayer for the Spirit's sevenfold gifts after the baptismal anointing with *myron* and a washing of the neophytes' feet. It cannot be ruled out that the "spiritual seal" is the sort of general prayer, without a hand laying or second anointing (forbidden by the Council of Orange in 441), which non-Roman bishops in the West often said at some point after the baptisms when they could, and which in southern Gaul is sometimes referred to as "confirmation": *confirmare neophytos.*[56]

This brings us to Roman evidence after AT. Crucial in this regard is the letter of Pope Innocent I (d. 417) to Bishop Decentius of Gubbio around 416 detailing Roman practice on several matters, one of which is the consignation of the newly baptized. Communications in Italy were being disrupted by barbarian invasions at this time, and Rome itself had been sacked by Visigoths in 410, a catastrophe which shocked the world. Of it Jerome said *capta est urbs quae totum cepit orbem*. To refute an outcry that it had happened due to Rome's forsaking its old gods (paganism in the City had finally been outlawed in 395) Augustine wrote *De Civitate Dei*. An indigenization of Christianity in Roman forms of language and art was under way in order to fill the vacuum caused by the withdrawal of imperial administration and Christian urbanity eastward to Constantinople after 330. The church of the left behind laid claim to Rome's classical heritage, shorn of its paganism, as one of its own reasons to be the unique source of culture and religion in a West facing dark days. Latin language, art, and architecture were being Christianized and were beginning to flourish under strong popes like Damasus, Leo, and Gregory, who dedicated themselves to making Roman Christianity paradigmatic for the West.[57]

One aspect of this effort in the face of appalling odds was the latinizing, stabilizing, and commending of Roman liturgical procedures to churches outside the City. This is what Innocent is doing in his letter to the bishop of Gubbio, a town in Perugia some hundred miles north of Rome. Concerning what happens liturgically to Roman neophytes after their baptism and chrismation Innocent is adamant that only bishops are involved. The reason for this is twofold. *Implicitly* it enhances the bishop's unique and indispensable role as the focus of unity in churches beset by the disintegrating effects of barbarian violence and as the touchstone of continuity with Western Christianity's past, which rests upon Rome's apostolic foundation by Peter and Paul, a theme which later reaches its peak with Leo I (440–461). *Explicitly* Innocent requires episcopal hegemony in consignation on the precedent of Acts 8, which recounts how the apostles Peter and John were sent from Jerusalem to Samaria to give by prayer and hand laying the Holy Spirit to those there who had already been baptized by Philip. Innocent concludes:

"It belongs solely to the episcopal office that bishops consign and give the Paraclete Spirit. This is proved not only by ecclesiastical custom but also by that reading of the Acts of the Apostles which recounts how Peter and John were directed to give the Holy Spirit to the already baptized."[58]

Innocent thus knows the "ecclesiastical custom" peculiar to AT 21 that associates prayer, hand laying, and anointing *in frontem* after baptism and its presbyteral chrismation exclusively with the bishop. This unit is the baptismal *missa* structure we have seen in AT 21, which was translated into Latin (the Verona version) around 350 when latinizing was beginning to gather force in the Roman church. But Innocent's accounting for this episcopal rite in terms of Acts 8 is new, selective, and awkward. It is new in that reference to Acts 8 is not made even in North Africa, where a pneumatic hand laying is already witnessed in the early third century by Tertullian, as we have seen.[59] It is selective in that Peter, a prime figure in Roman imagery, is said in Acts 10.44–48 and 11.14–18 to have been involved in incidents when as a result of his preaching to Gentiles the Holy Spirit came upon his hearers *before* their baptism rather than after it.[60] Innocent's choice of Acts 8 is therefore hardly dispassionate in the face of New Testament evidence. It is selective for reasons specific to his argument in its historical context. And it is awkward beyond those specific reasons in that, if one cared to be literal-minded, the baptized could be compared to Samaritans but for their consignation at episcopal hands. Worse, all baptisms could be compared to that of Philip and be said to require remedying by bishops as Philip's was by Peter and John. The argument can easily be forced to imply that the Holy Spirit does not come into the baptismal scenario until the bishop acts. This notion is at variance with the tradition we have noted stemming from Titus 3.5, John 3.5, and 1 Corinthians 12.13 into the Verona version of AT 21, and even into Gallican and Gelasian chrismation formulas.

Given all this in its historical setting, one must conclude that Innocent's letter to Decentius, at least on the matter of consignation, is propaganda rather than a serene and objective articulation of doctrine—well meaning, understandable in the circumstances, and for high motives, but propaganda nonetheless. Based on a selective biblical appeal, it seeks to justify a new understanding of an old post-chrismational structure in Roman baptismal procedure. It may be doubted that this understanding at Rome would antedate the Verona translation of AT, which does not support it, but we cannot say with certainty whether that translation of around 350 was known at Rome or not. Yet all signs point to AT 21's procedure having already entered Roman usage prior to this period. Innocent suggests this by referring to it as "ecclesiastical custom." The eighth century *Gelasian Sacramentary* confirms its continued presence in that usage, but altered along the lines Innocent witnesses. This suggests that someone prior to Innocent had altered the "Lord God" prayer of AT 21 into an epiclesis of the Holy Spirit. If one compares the Verona version of the prayer with that in the *Gelasian Sacramentary* (the next time the prayer surfaces in a liturgical book) it can be seen how

basically slight the original change in the prayer would
have had to be:

(Verona) AT 21	Gelasian
Lord God	Almighty God, Father of our Lord Jesus Christ,
you have made them worthy to receive remission of sins through the laver of regeneration of the Holy Spirit;	you have made your servants to be regenerated by water and the Holy Spirit, and have given them remission of all their sins;
send upon them your grace,	*pour upon them, Lord, your Holy Spirit, the Paraclete,*
that they may serve you according to your will.[61]	and give them the spirit of wisdom and understanding, etc.[62]

Verona's "send upon them your grace" has become in
the Gelasian redaction "pour upon them, Lord, your
Holy Spirit, the Paraclete." This change has to be one
known already by Innocent in the early fifth century
since it is what makes intelligible his pneumatic interpretation of the old prayer and his call on Acts 8 for
support.[63] It is a change the Verona translator seems
either not to know or to ignore around 350. It is thus
plausible that the change occurred sometime between
350 and 416, when Innocent wrote to Decentius. One
asks whether there were theological conditions during
this span which might have urged such a change.

During these years, in addition to local Roman concerns for latinization and ecclesiastical unity after the
plundering of the City in 410, a major theological issue
reached a head in both East and West. From around
360 the doctrine of the Holy Spirit had become acutely
controversial. A group of Arian theologians known as

59

Macedonians was maintaining the divinity of Christ but denying that of the Holy Spirit. Basil of Cappadocia (d. 379) was one of several who wrote against this heresy, and the second Ecumenical Council, at Constantinople in 381, among other things condemned Macedonianism and established the divinity of the Holy Spirit as authoritative teaching.[64] Jerome was present during the council, returning to Rome the following year where he gained employment as secretary and advisor to Pope Damasus until the latter's death in 384. During this time Jerome became acquainted with Innocent and was later supported by him in his monastic endeavors in Palestine after Innocent became pope in 401. In Palestine Jerome finished his translation of Didymus's *On the Holy Spirit*, a project he had begun at Rome under Damasus but discontinued on the pope's death.[65] At this same time Ambrose in Milan is listing the gifts of the Holy Spirit in the "invocation of the priest" at the "spiritual seal"— gifts the later *Gelasian Sacramentary* includes but which Innocent's letter to Decentius does not mention. Concern over the nature and role of the Holy Spirit was obviously present in major churches of the time.

The evidence is circumstantial but strong that AT's "Lord God" prayer in the baptismal *missa* was changed from an invocation of God's grace upon the neophytes to an epiclesis of the Holy Spirit around the time Jerome was in the City. But there are reasons which speak against Jerome himself being responsible for the change even as they point to the fact that the change occured around this time. Jerome, never one to hold back criticism when he thought it due, lampoons the notion that "from the bishop alone proceeds the calling down of the Holy Spirit" (*ad episcopi tantum imprecationem Spiritus sancti defluit*) and attributes the bishop's "running around" (*excurrat*) to lay hands on the baptized as "more to the honor of the priesthood than to the law of necessity" (*ad honorem potius sacerdotii quam ad legem necessitatis*). One might infer from this that Jerome's doctrine of baptism was not unlike that of the "Lord God" prayer. He surely has none of Innocent's view of consignation, although from his remarks it may be surmised that he has detected its beginnings and does not think very much of it.[66]

In the pneumatological climate before and after the Council of Constantinople there was generally heightened interest in the working of the Spirit in baptism, an interest which could hardly ignore Acts 8–9. Athanasius, Cyril of Jerusalem, Hilary of Poitiers, John Chrysostom, Epiphanius of Salamis, and Isidore of Pelusium and Optatus of Milevis in North Africa, all of them writers during this period, are inclined to associate giving the Spirit with hand laying during the apostolic era. But neither Athanasius of Alexandria, nor Chrysostom of Antioch and Constantinople, nor Cyril of Jerusalem mention this act as figuring in the baptismal procedure of their churches, where the baptismal chrismation rather than hand laying had come to signify the (messianic) gift of the Spirit. Epiphanius in Palestine and Cyprus, and Isidore in Egypt, both monastics who became bishops, explain hand laying as an episcopal prerogative based on Acts 8 much as Innocent does, perhaps to counter the growth in their areas of presbyters both blessing and using chrism to the exclusion of bishops from the rites of baptism.[67] There is some suggestion of this in Innocent's letter as well. The full text specifies that although presbyters may anoint *in capite*, that is, on the head at the postbaptismal chrismation as they had always done, bishops alone anoint *in frontem* (as AT 21 makes clear if for different reasons). It will be remembered that Damasus before 384, and the second Council of Carthage around 390, felt constrained to forbid presbyters from "reconciling" penitents.[68] All these concerns arise at a time when episcopal presidency at every liturgical event is breaking down and beginning to pass to presbyters, eliciting bishops' insistence on their own prerogatives. It appears to be pneumatological speculation stimulated by the Macedonian controversy as used at Rome to back up episcopal prerogatives in baptism with which Jerome disagrees.

Whatever else may be said of Innocent's context and reasons, he clearly makes the giving of the Holy Spirit distinct from and subsequent to what the "Lord God" prayer of AT 21 calls the *lauacrum regenerationis spiritus sancti*. He attributes this giving of the Spirit to the bishop's signing the neophyte on the forehead with chrism. And despite his appeal to Acts 8 and the apostolic hand laying reported there he does not even mention hand laying in his letter. What he derives from Acts 8 is episcopal hegemony in giving the Holy Spirit (what Jerome objects to earlier), but not the mode by which the apostles did this, namely, by hand laying. Paradoxically, this puts AT 21's procedure closer to that described in Acts 8 than it does Innocent's. AT 21 at least emphasizes the apostolic hand laying (*Episcopus vero manum illis inponens inuocet dicens. . . .*), adds the "oil of thanksgiving" to it with a Trinitarian formula, and seems if anything to make the signation *in frontem* a subordinate gesture the purpose of which is to refer back to the Trinitarian baptismal confession and its messianic anointing, as we have seen. What Innocent describes to Decentius thus does not conform entirely to Acts 8, to AT 21, to North African usage described by Tertullian, or to Ambrose's "spiritual seal." Nor does what he describes correspond to anything we know of in the liturgy of baptism in the various Eastern churches which by this period are coming to link the gift of the Spirit with the *presbyteral* chrismation after baptism. One asks what Innocent is up to.

What Innocent commends to Decentius is that he adopt a Roman liturgical procedure for concluding baptism which is structurally old, namely, the episcopal *missa* we have tried to identify in the Verona translation of AT 21. But Innocent does not distinguish earlier understanding of the old structure in Roman "ecclesiastical custom" from more recent interpretations of it, interpretations influenced by a half-century of pneumatological debate and perhaps by the growth at Rome of presbyteral consignation which was weakening the bishop's liturgical role in baptism and in the church. Innocent recommends that Decentius introduce the old Roman structure modified in light of these interpretations.

What Innocent does is a good example of bending liturgy to serve theology and current pastoral needs, something which usually ends with theology and current needs determining rather than interpreting liturgical text and form. *Interpreting* liturgical text and form is mystagogy, an old and respectable form of theological discourse.[69] But Innocent is not doing mystagogy here. He is theologically enhancing one element in the old *missa*, the episcopal signation *in frontem*, in such a way that it eventually will alter people's perception of the structure as a whole and even alter the structure itself. Even if the Verona version of the "Lord God" prayer had not already been changed into an epiclesis of the Holy Spirit by this time, Innocent's stress on the bishop's exclusive right to sign *in frontem*, and thus give the Holy Spirit to neophytes after their baptism, would require the change. Such a change we may see finally in the expanded version of AT's prayer by the time of the *Gelasian Sacramentary* some three centuries later.

But in the history of liturgical development structure often outlives meaning.[70] Elements are preserved even when their original meaning is lost under layers of subsequent interpretations. This *preservation tendency* is responsible for the survival of the old *missa* structure in modern rites of confirmation, where only the trained analytical eye is able to detect its underlying presence. Elements may also become detached from their original place and purpose, acquiring new and broader meanings in the process. This *universalizing tendency* is at work in the gradual detachment of the old *missa* structure from baptism during the medieval period, when it was perceived by theologians as an independent rite needing its own theology. It was this theology that opened it up to other interpretations such as its being a universal sacrament of Christian maturity or majority. Finally, elements are introduced which have no apparent relationships to others. This *arbitrary tendency* may be seen in the introduction of the Holy Spirit into the old *missa's* "Lord God" prayer. The prayer thus became an epiclesis around Innocent's time, making it seem as though the Holy Spirit had to be supplied *after* baptism by a second postbaptismal anointing *in frontem* at episcopal hands.

Of the three tendencies in liturgical development just mentioned, those of preservation and arbitrariness are evident in Innocent's letter to Decentius. The old *missa* structure is preserved, but its "Lord God" prayer is changed into an epiclesis of the Holy Spirit, and the signation with oil *in frontem* is enhanced as the episcopal prerogative par excellence. These two tendencies together make possible the universalizing tendency which will turn the old *missa* first into the Roman rite of consignation, as we can infer from Innocent and see in the *Gelasian Sacramentary*. As this rite merges with Gallican practices of episcopal oversight of baptism, it gives rise to medieval and later rites of confirmation separated from baptism which are practiced in wide and equivocal variety in many Western churches today.

3. NEW PERSPECTIVES

The purpose of structural analysis of liturgical units is to understand how the unit works. The analyst asks *what* it is that is at work and *how* this is accomplished. Answers to these questions aid both fundamental understanding and historical reconstruction as well. Understanding and reconstruction in turn may allow a new intelligibility framework to emerge, enabling us to see accustomed things in a fresh and perhaps sharper focus. This is what Einstein did for Newtonian physics.[71]

Here we have tried to analyze an early liturgical unit, the *missa*, in terms of its structure and to note the regularity with which it turns up in both East and West as the formal ending of offices, the formal ending of eucharistic Word services, the formal ending of monastic synaxes of prayer and perhaps as the form of monastic communion from the reserved sacrament, and as the solemn episcopal conclusion of baptism in the Verona version of AT 21. That the *missa* structure is the basis of later Roman consignation, and of medieval and modern confirmation, is an unprecedented suggestion. It is also one which the evidence so far adduced seems to support even though it calls into question the conventional presumptions to which we have become accustomed in trying to account for the origin, development, and meaning of this controverted rite. Should our analysis of confirmation's origins in the *missa* structure stand the tests of criticism, our view might permit a fresh intelligibility framework which could clarify certain matters.

First, by anchoring the origin of confirmation in the *missa* structure it becomes easier to see that what some Eastern churches have come to call "confirmation"in their baptismal liturgies is in fact not a rite of confirmation at all because no underlying *missa* is in evidence. What one sees in them is an entirely different struc-

65

ture, namely, the standard postbaptismal chrismation by a presbyter. The original messianic and christic meaning of this chrismation began to modulate into a pneumatic key in late fourth-century Jerusalem and had become entirely pneumatic, at least among the Byzantines, by the eighth century, as we have seen. There is therefore no confirmation rite in Eastern usages, but a pneumaticized postbaptismal chrismation by a presbyter such as we see in its more archaic messianic-christic form in AT 21 just before the episcopal *missa* begins. Eastern chrismation is the structural equivalent of the Roman postbaptismal chrismation by a presbyter *in capite*, not of the Roman episcopal *missa* with its second chrismation *in frontem*.

Second, in similar fashion neither can one affirm a *missa* structure in Hispano-Gallican liturgies of baptism. What the liturgical evidence suggests is that these liturgies originally followed Eastern rather than Roman procedure, namely, baptism in water followed by a single chrismation by a presbyter or deacon. At that point or later a bishop might "confirm" or otherwise ratify the baptism by an act which had more of a disciplinary than a sacramental character. We know this because no rite for such a ratification ever appears in the liturgical books themselves. Local synods only allude to what bishops did in exceptional cases when the integrity of a baptism or the status of a putatively baptized person was in question—in the first case by a hand laying or "blessing," in the second (for heretics) by a hand laying *ut accipiat Spiritum*, apparently without any prayer being said. Winkler points out that, when Gallican bishops are said in non-liturgical sources to "confirm neophytes" (*confirmare neophytos*), there is no liturgical evidence that they performed a rite involving hand laying with prayer for the Holy Spirit.[72] We can only estimate that this episcopal act in Spain and Gaul begins to be associated with the Holy

Spirit for the first time in a Pentecost homily attributed to Faustus of Riez around 450, although it may be later.[73] In any case, certain elements of this homily become standard for later perception since medieval canonists mistakenly attributed it to the early fourth-century Pope Melchiades and thus invested it with high authority. To this homily we shall return presently.

Third, if our analysis is correct it suggests a three-stage origin for modern confirmation. *Stage one* is the report in AT 21 of a typical *missa* involving non-pneumatic prayer and coming under the bishop's hand. It is the prerogative of the bishop, who is said to do nothing else in baptism except bless and exorcize the oils, and it is his peculiar liturgy for the newly baptized. As such it is redolent of what had just happened to them in the *lauacrum regenerationis spiritus sancti*, as the bishop's "Lord God" prayer calls their baptism and anointing. He also anoints them by a hand laying and signation on the forehead in the name of the Trinity. His prayer for them is unipartite, as was that of their catechist (AT 19) and of himself at their last exorcism (AT 20). This formally and publicly concludes the baptismal event of washing and anointing; it releases the neophytes into the assembly which must then redeploy itself before beginning the baptismal eucharist.

Stage two is witnessed by Innocent's interpretation of the customary episcopal *missa* in light of the theological and disciplinary climate in the church of Rome between 380 and 416. He emphasizes the already old episcopal hegemony in performing the *missa* but now links this to Acts 8, insisting that the hegemony stems not only from the "ecclesiastical custom" of his church, but also from a scriptural warrant that makes the bishop the only one who can give the Holy Spirit, *pace* Jerome and the East. This suggests that the old *missa's* "Lord God" prayer had already been transformed into an epiclesis of the Holy Spirit, perhaps resembling the form we find in the later Gelasian Sacramentary. The no doubt unintended effect of this was to open a breach in initiatory sequence and theology, separating the Spirit from baptism and locating its invocation and giving to the episcopal *missa*, now referred to by Innocent as consignation.

Stage three is the gradual merging of this Roman practice with the Hispano-Gallican practice of episcopal disciplinary oversight of baptism, an oversight which seems more often than not to have been exercised well after the baptisms had taken place.[74] In ninth-century Gaul this Romanized "confirmation" is mentioned as being administered, even when a bishop *was* present for Easter baptism, either *after communion* at the baptismal eucharist or *a week later* on the octave day of Easter. At Rome itself, on the contrary, the unity of Christian initiation seems to have been preserved at least until the twelfth century.[75] Separating confirmation from baptism in Gaul widened chronologically the theological breach between baptism and the giving of the Holy Spirit witnessed by Innocent. The old *missa* of baptism, which became Innocent's "consignation," becomes "confirmation" from the sixth to the ninth centuries in Gaul. This evolution, accomplished by the gradual adoption of Roman elements into Gallican liturgies over a span of some three centuries, forced out older Gallican practices of "confirmation" and placed their Roman successor more and more subsequent to baptism itself—separated first by the baptismal eucharist, then by Easter week, and finally by the time it took for a circuit-riding Gallic bishop to make his rural rounds.

The breach between baptism and the giving of the Holy Spirit, which is evidenced in germ in Innocent's letter to Decentius, is ideologically clearer in the hom-

68

ily attributed to Faustus of Riez and receives there a new symbolic justification:

"In baptism we are born anew for life, after baptism we are confirmed for battle (*confirmamur ad pugnam*); in baptism we are washed, after baptism we are strengthened (*post baptismum roboramur*)."[76]

This more definite sequestering of the effects of baptism from those of Innocent's consignation gives a new sort of prophylactic symbolism to the latter (a symbolism earlier associated with prebaptismal exorcisms and anointing with the oil of catechumens). Such a view may have led to expanding the epicletic form of the old "Lord God" prayer by listing the Spirit's gifts from Isaiah 11.2f, as we see in the Gelasian Sacramentary[77] and in later medieval authors and liturgical texts.[78]

4. THE ORIGINS OF CONFIRMATION
To summarize, the origins of modern confirmation seem to proceed in the following stages:

1. The third-century baptismal *missa* of AT 21, which did not originally contain a prayer for the Holy Spirit and had as its main ceremonial gesture a coming of each of the neophytes under the bishop's hand.

2. The fifth-century reinterpretation of the old *missa* witnessed by Innocent I, in which prayer is made by the bishop for the Holy Spirit to be given in a ceremonial gesture of signation on the forehead of each of the neophytes.

3. The sixth to ninth-century Romanizing and sacramentalizing of Hispano-Gallican practices of episcopal disciplinary oversight of baptism known as "confirmation of neophytes." This merging process separated consignation from baptism and gave

it a universalizing prophylactic emphasis together with the name "confirmation."

By the third stage, when confirmation has become separated from baptism, often by some years, it would no longer be entirely clear what the original liturgical structure or intent might have been. It is no wonder that modern authors, moving back through this later evidence in which structural and intentional questions about origins are neither asked nor answered, finally come upon AT 21 with the orientations of medieval theology, the Faustus homily, and the letter of Innocent I fixed in their minds. They fall into anachronisms, chief among which is finding confirmation in AT 21 either in its medieval or fifth-century form of consignation, but oddly tacked on to baptism. Such a stance often results in evidence being forced, as when the "Lord God" prayer in the Verona translation of AT 21 is declared corrupt and then rewritten in light of other translations made centuries later.

The fact is that *confirmation* is not in AT 21, the main early source of later Roman initiatory practice. What is there is an archaic episcopal *missa* of neophytes from their baptism into their first eucharist where the Holy Spirit strengthens their "faith in truth" for Divine Service. This is something that will be reiterated each time they commune sacramentally for the rest of their lives in the *ecclesia*, where the Spirit flourishes. The Spirit is the first and greatest gift of the Anointed One in whom they were washed and anointed for the forgiveness of their sins by the bath of regeneration of the Holy Spirit. The revelation of Jesus as this Anointed One is consummated by the Holy Spirit in baptism. It is this deeply mysterious event which is marshalled in such a way as to transform catechumens into faithful and to hold them in its grip—just as the event of the first Pentecost transformed a diversity of folks into a People devoting themselves to apostolic teaching and fellowship, to the breaking of bread and prayers (Acts 2).[79]

Innocent I witnesses a shift which begins the long process of separating the Holy Spirit from this constitutive Christian event in the West. This process begins paradoxically, with Innocent's emphasizing, even aggrandizing, the coming of the Spirit at the bishop's hand in a liturgical structure subsequent to baptism. This move not only focuses but also limits the Spirit, and when this practice later merges with Gallican disciplinary preoccupations the focus and limitation are tightened still more. Reallocated symbolism, such as the defensive and prophylactic images we see in Faustus, begins to accumulate and eventually includes cultural images of enfranchisement, majority, and even puberty. These images in turn fuel theological speculations on how baptismal grace may be said to increase, especially at certain ages. Educationalism casts its syllabuses to correspond with and to foster these age-contexts until, finally, confirmation's administration comes to be determined not on the basis of baptism but on the basis of modern educational sequence.

As Nathan Mitchell observes, even the most perceptive theologians eventually no longer understood how the symbolic cluster associated with giving the Holy Spirit relates to the symbolic cluster associated with baptismal transformation and incorporation into Christ. The result was finally to give a rationale for the separation of baptismal and confirmational symbol clusters. "The 'law of accumulated symbolism,' " he says, "has done its work: the heavy symbolism of Christian initiation has, under the influence of declining catechesis and theological misunderstanding, forced the original architecture of the rite to collapse into two 'separate and distinct sacraments' with 'separate and distinct effects.' "[80]

The foregoing attempt to clarify the origins of modern confirmation makes it possible to look critically at its recent reform.

NOTES

1. See J.A. Jungmann, *The Mass of the Roman Rite* 2.427–432.

2. "Confirmation: A Suggestion from Structure," *Worship* 58 (1984) 386–395. For a response see Frank C. Quinn, "Confirmation Reconsidered: Rite and Meaning," *Worship* 59 (1985) 354–369.

3. Cuming, 20; Dix, 38–39, where the "confirmation" section is numbered 22:1–5; Botte, 52–54.

4. Dix, xl.

5. See Kavanagh, *The Shape of Baptism* 10–11; G.W.H. Lampe, *The Seal of the Spirit* (London 1967) 82–91.

6. The prebaptismal anointing in East Syria, as G. Winkler has pointed out, is never called "seal" (*hatma*) but "sign" or "mark" (*rushma*), and its significance is messianic rather than covenantal. I summarize the evidence in *The Shape of Baptism* 40–42. The East Syrian *rushma* is clearly not confirmation, despite Dix's assertion that the "Syrian Church down to c.A.D. 650 administered 'the seal' of Confirmation *before* Baptism . . . other churches after;" xl. See G. Winkler, "The Original Meaning of the Prebaptismal Anointing and Its Implications," *Worship* 52 (1978) 24–25.

7. E.g., J.D.C. Fisher, *Confirmation Then and Now* (London 1978).

8. Summarized in *The Shape of Baptism* 14–31.

9. Thomas Marsh, *Gift of Community: Baptism and Confirmation* (Wilmington 1984), discussed in F. Quinn, *art. cit. passim.*

10. A good review of recent reforms and discussions is in Gerard Austin, *Anointing With the Spirit. The Rite of Confirmation: The Use of Oil and Chrism* (New York 1985).

11. For the important distinction between first and second order discourse and its ramifications for methodology when it comes to understanding liturgy see my *On Liturgical Theology* (New York 1985).

12. In Botte's edition, where the early Latin text is given in full, the baptismal section takes 64 lines. Confirmation by contrast needs only 24. Botte 44–54.

13. Cuming 19–20. Dix 38; Botte 50.

14. Justin, 1 Apology 61, some two generations earlier calls it only "a place where there is water."

15. Botte 54.

16. Cuming 17; Dix 30; Botte 40. This catechumenal dismissal from instruction is not unique in AT. It can be seen in later liturgical documents, where a specific prayer text and hand laying are specified. In the eighth century Barberini Euchologion, reflecting earlier Byzantine usage, such a structure is used when an infant catechumen receives its name on the eighth day after birth, and in the rite for the "making of a catechumen"; see *Rituale Armenorum*, ed. F.C. Conybeare (Oxford 1905) 388, 390–391. The same catechumenal dismissal structure, with a different prayer, is specified in a thirteenth century Armenian order for an infant catechumen on the eighth day after birth; see Conybeare 88. One suspects that these prayers originally belonged to a repertoire of prayers for dismissing catechumens at the end of instruction sessions which, after the demise of the catechumenate in Middle Eastern churches, were reallocated to other events centering on infants. Here they survive with their hand laying still intact.

17. We note that *Ungueo te oleo sancto in nomine Ie(s)u Chr(ist)i* is a declaration, not a prayer, and that it is messianic, not pneumatic.

18. Botte 52.

19. Cuming 20. Dix 38; Botte 52: *D(omi)ne D(eu)s, qui dignos fecisti eos remissionem mereri peccatorum per lauacrum regenerationis sp(irit)us s(an)c(t)i, inmitte in eos tuam gratiam, ut*

tibi seruiant secundum uoluntatem tuam; quoniam tibi est gloria,
etc.

20. Cuming 20. Dix 39; Botte 52: *Ungueo te s(an)c(t)o oleo in*
d(omi) no patre omnipotente et Chr(ist)o Ie(s)u et sp(irit)u
s(an)c(t)o.

21. Cuming 21. Dix 39; Botte 54.

22. Botte 52.

23. The grammar of the *Episcopus uero* sentence is notable.
Its main verb is *inuocet:* the bishop *prays.* The participles
inponens and *dicens* are subordinate to this. Their sequence in
Latin, and probably in the original Greek, does not necessarily imply chronological sequence, namely, that the bishop
first lays hands on each and then prays for all. *Dicens* comes
last only because a quote of what the bishop is to say (the
"Lord God" prayer) immediately follows. There are, in other
words, not *two* handlayings, one before the "Lord God"
prayer and another after it at the anointing and signation,
but only *one* at the latter point. Similarly, the phrase *offerat*
osculum et dicat at the rite's end does not mean the kiss takes
place first, followed by the greeting, but that kiss and greeting go together.

24. Cuming 21; Dix 40–43; Botte 54–58.

25. Cuming 18; Dix 34; Botte 46. This section of AT comes
not from the Verona text, where there is a lacuna, but from
a seventh century Sahidic translation of a Greek text to
which elements were added after the Council of Constantinople in 381. See Cuming 19 note 1; Dix 35; Botte 46–47.

26. See Cuming 20. Dix 38 regards the Verona text as corrupt; Botte 53 thinks a line has been left out in either the
Latin translation or its Greek predecessor, and he recon-
structs what he thinks it ought to have been.

27. G.W.H. Lampe, *The Seal of the Spirit* 138–141. Dix later
had misgivings about labelling this section of AT 21 "confirmation" (see Cuming 20), and Botte regarded his rewriting
of Verona at this point as nothing more than conjecture;
Lampe 139–140.

28. The Sahidic translation of AT was done before 700 but contains no prayer texts; see Cuming 6.

29. *De Sacramentis* 2.24; see Whitaker 120.

30. *Omnipotens sempiterne Deus, qui regenerare dignatus es hos famulos . . . ex aqua et spiritu sancto, quique dedisti eis remissionem omnium peccatorum . . .* See Whitaker 178; Lampe 141, note 1.

31. Missale Gallicanum Vetus: *Infusio chrismae. Deus pater domini nostri Jesu Christi, qui te regeneravit ex aqua et spiritu sancto, qui tibi dedit remissionem peccatorum, ipse te linit . . . ;* PL 72.369. Bobbio Missal: *Suffundis Chrisma . . . dicens: Deus pater domini nostri Jesu Christi qui te regeneravit per aquam et spiritum sanctum . . . tibi dedit remissionem peccatorum per lavacrum regenerationis et sanguinem, ipse te liniat . . .* See Whitaker 202. The Stowe Missal is similar; Whitaker 210.

32. Quinn, *art. cit.* 357, 360–361. But see Lampe 142–143. That terms such as *perficere* and *consummare* imply the addition of something new, as Quinn maintains, is dubious.

33. Cuming 10–11; Dix 7–9; Botte 12–16.

34. Cuming 11. The Latin (Botte 16) is difficult and its authenticity is doubted by Dix and Botte, but Cuming thinks it "quite credible."

35. Cuming 21; Dix 40–42 without textual warrant heads the section "The Paschal Mass"; Botte 54–58. On the question of when baptism was associated with Easter see T. Talley, *The Origins of the Liturgical Year* 33–37.

36. AT 4 in Cuming 11; Dix 8–9; Botte 16. "To minister to you" is *tibi ministrare* in Verona, *hierateuein soi* in Greek versions.

37. AT 1–8 in Cuming 8–13; Dix 2–18; Botte 4–27.

38. Cuming 29; Dix 62; Botte 88.

39. *The Apostolic Tradition of Hippolytus* (Cambridge 1934) 93; see Lampe 136–137.

40. Thus Lampe 137.

41. See A. Winkler, *Das armenische Initiationsrituale: Entwicklungsgeschichtliche und liturgievergleichende Untersuchung der Quellen des 3. bis 10. Jahrhunderts* (OCA 217, Rome 1982) 135–165 *passim*.

42. The preceding sentences express a doctrine of Christ from Galatians 3.27, Ephesians 1.5, Philippians 3.21, Hebrews 3.15. Into him the neophytes have been engrafted and "made Christs by receiving the emblem of the Holy Spirit" as they undergo representationally the act of baptism by taking "the part of Christ." Whitaker 26.

43. In Whitaker 26–27, from Cyril's *Mystagogical Catechesis* 3, based on a lection of 1 John 2.20–28. I have slightly modernized the language.

44. In Conybeare 405; Whitaker 73. Pneumatic emphasis tends to drive out or supersede messianic emphasis in baptism. We shall see this later in the reformed Roman rite of adult initiation of 1972, where pneumatic confirmation knocks out the messianic postbaptismal chrismation; and in the reformed rite of confirmation of 1971, where the formula of administration is that of the *Barberini Euchologion's* pneumatic chrismation.

45. Cyprian *Epistle* 73 to Januarius; Tertullian *De Baptismo* 8.1, *De Resurrectione Carnis* 8 (Whitaker 9); Augustine *Sermon* 324 (Whitaker 96).

46. Ambrose *De Sacramentis* 3.1–8 (Whitaker 121).

47. Whitaker 144–148.

48 See note 31.

49. Thus A. Winkler, "Confirmation or Chrismation? A Study in Comparative Liturgy," *Worship* 58 (1984) 2–17.

50. See Quinn 360–361; Winkler 12.

51. Arles 9; Quinn 360. Canon 7 of I Constantinople (381) reconciles heretics by an anointing of the senses and the words, "The seal of the gift of the Holy Spirit," Schaff-Wace 14. 185.

52. Quinn 362.

53. Tertullian is definite: *Dehinc manus imponitur per benedictionem advocans et invitans Spiritum Sanctum;* see Whitaker 9.

54. *De Mysteriis* 42; see Whitaker 123.

55. *De Sacramentis* 3.1; Whitaker 120.

56. See Winkler 8–13, who cautions against reading Gallican evidence according to Roman presuppositions at this early date.

57. See Richard Krautheimer, *Rome: Profile of a City* (Princeton 1980) 33–58.

58. *Hoc autem pontificium solis debere episcopis, ut vel consignent, vel Paracletum Spiritum tradant, non solum consuetudo ecclesiastica demonstrat, verum et illa lectio Actuum Apostolorum, quae asserit Petrum et Ioannem esse directos, qui iam baptizatis traderent Spiritum Sanctum.* Epistle 25.3 (PL 56.515).

59. See note 53.

60. I comment on New Testament baptismal sequence, and on what one can and cannot make out of it, in *The Shape of Baptism* 16–20.

61. Cuming 20; Dix 38 (where it is made an epiclesis); Botte 52. See Lampe 140–141.

62. Whitaker 178, modernized. In *The Shape of Baptism* 66, I compared both these texts as epicleses, following Dix and Botte on AT's original form, which I should not have done.

63. It will be recalled that similar wording in the prayer does not appear in Arabic and Ethiopic translations of AT until the thirteenth century.

64. Schaff-Wace 14.172.

65. J.N.D. Kelly, *Jerome: His Life, Writings, and Controversies* (New York 1975) 142. On Jerome's relationship with Damasus see 82–90; on Innocent's backing see 322–323.

66. See Lampe 199.

67. Lampe 224–226.

68. See Chapter One 15–16.

69. For an excellent essay on mystagogy see Robert Taft, "The Liturgy of the Great Church: An Initial Synthesis of Structure and Interpretation on the Eve of Iconoclasm," *Dumbarton Oaks Papers* 34–35 (1982) 45–75.

70. Thus Robert Taft, "The Structural Analysis of Liturgical Units: An Essay in Methodology," *Beyond East and West: Problems in Liturgical Understanding* 151–164, especially 152.

71. See Taft, "The Structural Analysis of Liturgical Units: An Essay in Methodology," 152–153.

72. "Confirmation or Chrismation" 12–13. So too L.L. Mitchell, *Baptismal Anointing* (London 1966) 125.

73. Thus Winkler 13.

74. See M. Andrieu, *Le Pontifical romain au moyen-âge*, vol. 1 (Vatican City 1938) 246–247.

75. Nathan Mitchell, "Dissolution of the Rite of Christian Initiation," *Made, Not Born* (Notre Dame 1976) 55–56; Kavanagh, *The Shape of Baptism* 67–68.

76. Winkler 14.

77. Whitaker 178.

78. N. Mitchell 57–69.

79. Kavanagh, *The Shape of Baptism* 22–23.

80. See N. Mitchell 71–72.

Reform

Chapter Three

The Reform of Confirmation

The reform of confirmation which resulted from the
Second Vatican Council cannot be grasped adequately
except in view of a larger reform of which it is a part.
That larger reform was of Christian initiation itself,
said by the Council's Constitution on the Liturgy,
Sacrosanctum Concilium (CL) 64–71, to be a *restoration*
which was to be carried out in such a way that the
sacraments of baptism, confirmation, and eucharist
should be clearly related and integrated. This outlook
is fundamental. The conciliar reform is a restoration
meant to reintegrate the various parts of Christian initiation which, as we have seen, had over the centuries
become separated from each other and had thus lost
intelligibility. The Council's purpose was therefore not
to introduce novelty but to restore relationships and to
foster the intellgibility those regained relationships
might yield.

Now that the 1983 Code of Canon Law has come into
effect this point is even more important. The new
Code's canons touching liturgy and sacraments do not
reiterate the myriad specific changes, which are contained in the liturgical books themselves, but the general norms and fundamental outlook laid down by the
Council. To know these norms in both their conciliar
and canonical modes of expression is an essential condition for interpreting the specific reforms contained in
the liturgical books. Such knowledge allows one to see
the trees without forgetting the forest to which they

belong. The three bodies of literature, conciliar, liturgical, and canonical, are meant to function as checks and balances on each other for the coherence and well being of the Church universal and local.

1. THE INITIATORY REFORM IN GENERAL

It must be remembered that the Council's fundamental outlook on initiation mentioned above, although contained *in globo* in CL 64–71, is not exhausted there. Since CL was the Council's first item of business to be completed and receive approval it strongly influenced other documents which were to follow. Some of these later documents expanded the fundamental outlook on initiation first expressed in CL. The dogmatic constitution on the Church, *Lumen Gentium* 3–14, stressed the priority of faith and baptism and the need for catechumens to be received with open arms. The decree on missions, *Ad Gentes* 13, develops this and details how catechumens are to be treated by the whole community which receives them for baptism. The developed conciliar outlook extends the intelligible reintegration of the sacraments of initiation to the whole process by which one comes to faith by conversion under grace, restoring the catechumenate throughout the Church (not just in "mission countries"), emphasizing evangelization as preparatory for catechesis, and urging the crucial priority of all this in the Church's life in view of the New Testament doctrines of conversion to God through Christ by the Holy Spirit.

To reduce this fundamental outlook on Christian initiation to practicable liturgical procedures was the charge given to the postconciliar *Consilium ad Exsequendam Constitutionem de Sacra Liturgia* and its forty *coetus*, or study groups, which were to draft specific liturgical reforms. *Coetus* 22 and 23 were assigned to overhaul the Roman Ritual, which contained the baptismal rites. *Coetus* 20 dealt with the Roman Pontifical, which contained the rite of confirmation. Illustrative of its sensitivity to its mandate to restore and integrate, the Consilium in October 1964 approved a set of principles submitted by *coetus* 22 which proposed that the reform of the Ritual should begin not with infant but adult baptism. The salient reasons for this were:

"In the case of adults is most clearly shown: (a) the character of baptism, in that it is a sacrament of faith according to the theology of the sacraments accepted in the Constitution on the Sacred Liturgy (CL 59); (b) the unity of Christian initiation as in article (CL 71) of the Constitution; (c) the coordination of baptism and the paschal celebration, which is mentioned in article (CL 109) of the Constitution . . . The entire rite of infants, however reformed, will have its roots in the adult rite from which it will have been derived, and not vice versa."[1]

The rite for adults had already gone through four of its twelve drafts by 1966 when the rite for infants, which would go through nine drafts in constant reference to the adult rite, was begun. Work on the rite of confirmation began in late 1967 and was finished in early 1970. Thus the developing rite of initiation of adults was undertaken first to serve as paradigm for the rites of infant baptism and confirmation, even though the three rites came to be published in reversed order; the rite for infants in 1969, the rite of confirmation in 1971, and the rite of adult initiation in 1972.

It cannot be doubted that the Consilium followed its conciliar mandate and put the rite of adult initiation at the center of all its initiatory reforms as the norm according to which all other aspects of initiation would be judged, especially disciplinary questions such as who is minister of confirmation. The norm also provides perspective in exceptional situations such as the reception of an already baptized adult into communion and what to do when the sacraments of initiation are celebrated separately for serious cause. The *Rite of Christian Initiation of Adults* translated the Council's fundamental outlook into basic procedures meant to restore and reintegrate the sacraments which crown the whole grace-laden way of coming to ecclesial faith for the whole Church.

The Council's fundamental outlook, thus translated into liturgical norms, forms the basis upon which the 1983 Code of Canon Law legislates concerning initiatory matters. These canons distill into legal form both the conciliar and liturgical modes of initiatory expression. Meant for universal application in the Latin Church, the general nature of the new canons presumes that their interpreters have a firm grasp on the conciliar and liturgical literature upon which the canons rest. Sacramental and liturgical matters in general are treated by the new Code in a section entitled "The Office of Sanctifying in the Church," canons 834–1253. The first part of this section is on the sacraments (840–1165); the second part deals with other acts of divine worship (1166–1204); the third part with sacred times and places (1205–1253).

The canons on the sacraments begin appropriately with initiatory matters in line with the statement in canon 842:2, "The sacraments of baptism, confirmation, and the most holy Eucharist are so interrelated [*inter se coalescunt*] that they are required for full Christian initiation." The authentic initiatory sequence which is fundamental to sacramental interrelatedness and intelligibility is baptism-confirmation-eucharist. This is consistently reiterated from CL 64–71 to the very design of the 1972 *Rite of Christian Initiation of Adults* and on into the 1983 Code. In canon 849 baptism is called "the gate to the sacraments"; in canon 879 confirmation is said to continue the path of Christian initiation; in canon 897 the eucharist is said to be "the summit and source of all Christian worship and life" to which all sacraments and apostolic works are closely related and directed. These statements, far from being static and self-contained, are relational and presume a dynamic progression from baptism and all that leads up to it, through confirmation as a continuation of what was begun in baptism, to eucharist as the summit and source of initiation no less than of all the other sacraments and of ecclesial life as a whole. Council, liturgy, and canon law insist without equivocation that the integrated sequence of the sacraments of initiation is both central and pivotal to understanding Christian life lived in a Church which sanctifies only because it is first sanctified by grace, faith, and sacraments.

The sequence of initiatory sacraments is thus not merely an obsession of the ecclesiastically tidy nor of liturgical fundamentalists. The sequence of interrelated sacraments is crucial for that full intelligibility necessary to provide a firm anchor for understanding the full sweep of what Christian life in the Church involves. It is precisely this to which the *Rite of Christian Initiation of Adults* 34 refers when it says:

"According to the ancient practice maintained in the Roman liturgy, *an adult is not to be baptized unless he receives confirmation immediately afterward*, provided no serious obstacles exist. This connection signifies the unity of the paschal mystery, the close connection [*necessitudo*] between the mission of the Son and the pouring out of the Holy Spirit, and the joint celebration of the sacraments by which the Son and the Spirit come with the Father upon the baptized."[2]

Here one detects that "coordination of baptism and the paschal celebration" mentioned in CL 109, the "unity of Christian initiation" mentioned in CL 71, and a theology of the sacraments alluded to generally in CL 59—in other words, all three of the reasons stated by *coetus* 22 in 1965 for placing the rite of adult initiation at the center of its reforms. One must also infer from this deeply traditional reiteration that sacramental sequence is crucial in initiation for reasons of the most important theological kind, namely, a realized trinitarianism at the common genesis of Christian identity and ecclesial existence. In this view, to confirm anyone at whatever age apart from the closest possible reference to baptism, or to make a practice of confirming only well after the eucharist has begun to be received, is to render less than necessary the relationship between the missions of Son and Spirit, to occlude the way in which Son and Spirit come with the Father upon the baptized, and to sunder the paschal mystery.

The matter is therefore of the first order of magnitude, so that to do something different is restricted to situations which are compelled only by *serious* reasons. Neither conventions to the contrary, nor convenience, nor educational fashions constitute serious reasons. In view of its theological stance, by "serious obstacle" paragraph 34 means a situation in which nothing else can be done. One does what one must. One may not do merely what one chooses. The general breadth and liberality of the initiatory reforms leave local churches much room to do prudently what they must, but they may not ignore initiatory sequence at the risk of overturning the tradition by sundering the unity of the paschal mystery or obfuscating the trinitarian foundation of the grace of ecclesial faith by which the Church claims to be sanctified and sanctifying. The case for change in the sequence of baptism-confirmation-eucharist must be argued against this standard. Change is neither an axiomatic first principle nor a foregone conclusion.

If sequence is important for baptism and confirmation, it is absolutely crucial when it comes to the eucharist in relation to the first two initiatory sacraments, for it is the eucharist alone which completes Christian initiation. Both baptism and confirmation stand necessarily open to being consummated in the eucharist and are directed to it (canon 897). The most immediate vocation of the baptized and confirmed is to stand before God in worship at the Table. For this reason the *Rite of Confirmation* 11 insists that those who are confirmed should receive communion in the same service:

"Adult catechumens and children who are baptized at an age when they are old enough for catechesis should ordinarily be admitted to confirmation and the eucharist at the same time they receive baptism . . . Similarly, adults who were baptized in infancy should, after suitable preparation, receive confirmation and eucharist in a common celebration."[3]

Even less ambiguously paragraph 13 states:

"Ordinarily confirmation takes place within Mass in order to express more clearly the fundamental connection of this sacrament with the entirety of Christian initiation.[4] The latter reaches its culmination in the communion of the body and blood of Christ. The newly confirmed should therefore participate in the eucharist which completes their Christian initiation."[5]

The liturgical norm is clear: the sacraments of initiation are regularly and ordinarily celebrated together beginning with baptism and culminating in eucharist. Separating them, not to say altering their sequence by anticipating eucharist before confirmation, requires serious reason or grave cause. This means that when those baptized in infancy come to be confirmed, at whatever age, they should receive their first communion immediately following. It is this principle which governs the Consilium's position on the age at which such persons are to be confirmed, as we shall see.

For the present, however, it must be pointed out that in the whole strategy of the postconciliar reform an initiatory sequence which does not end regularly and ordinarily in first communion is severely abnormal, a *ritus interruptus* which cannot but cause serious warps in theology and pastoral practice. Thus the relatively recent custom of delaying confirmation to later years has led to admitting young children to the eucharist prior to their confirmation. This in turn has led to making the sacrament of penance, instead of confirmation, the standard overture to first communion for children, a practice not without its critics among theologians and religious educators. The practice is sacramentally most abnormal, which makes it unlikely that satisfactory rationales for it will be forthcoming. The practice furthermore loosens confirmation from its baptismal and eucharistic frame, allowing it to begin to occlude baptism as the sacrament of true entry into the Church and to detract from the eucharist as the perennial sacrament of Christian "maturity" par excellence. And with the insertion of penance into confirmation's traditional place before first communion for children baptized in infancy the initiatory continuum would lose coherence as a unitary sequence and become unintelligible to many, theologians no less than bishops and religious educators.[6] It has been often forgotten that confirmation, so far from being a sovereign and self-contained sacrament, is held in being by two powerful and overlapping gravitational fields, so to speak. One is that exerted by baptism, the other by eucharist. Weaken either of these two fields and confirmation flies out of orbit and is in danger of mutating into something alien to the tradition.

2. THE REFORM OF CONFIRMATION

This was the problem faced by the initiatory *coetus* of the Consilium. Confirmation had come to be almost invariably celebrated apart from baptism and, more recently, well after the eucharist had already begun to be received by many of those who would be confirmed in childhood or adolescence. Such practice suggested that confirmation had some sort of autonomy which permitted it to fill a variety of needs: a puberty rite for young adolescents, a maturity rite for older adolescents or youth, a graduation rite from one or another grade in school.

The reform of confirmation therefore had to be considerable, even radical, lest the entire coherence of the initiatory reform crumble under the ambiguities and paradoxes which had grown up around this sacrament. In order to restore confirmation more intimately to baptism, as one can see in the rite of adult initiation's requirement that it follow immediately on baptism of adults and children of catechetical age,[7] the centuries-old restriction of confirming to episcopal ministry has been considerably loosened.[8] Presbyters who baptize such persons in the bishop's absence may now by law, not merely by occasional delegation, confirm them in the same service, and they may also associate other presbyters with them in doing so (canon 882). This is but one example of how unprecedented the reforms of confirmation had to be in order to fulfill the mandate of CL 71:

"The rite of Confirmation is to be revised, and the intimate connection which this sacrament has with the whole of Christian initiation is to be more clearly set forth . . . ."

Even more unprecedented were reforms of the very core of confirmation itself.

a. Divinae Consortium Naturae of Paul VI (1971)[9]

In this Apostolic Constitution introducing the reformed rite of confirmation Paul VI (the text is said to have been written mainly by Dom Botte) specified that the sacrament is conferred by an anointing with chrism on the forehead, the effect of which is a sealing with the gift of the Spirit. The document embodies a résumé of teachings about baptism and confirmation, avoiding controversy and maintaining throughout the necessity of keeping confirmation in the closest possible contact with baptism in order to sustain confirmation's intelligibility.

The document acknowledges that "In many Eastern rites, it seems that from early times a rite of anointing, not then clearly distinguished from baptism, prevailed for the conferring of the Holy Spirit." It also avoids calling such a rite of anointing "confirmation," confining this designation only to Western usages without formally distinguishing the equivocal ways in which the term has been used in different places over the centuries. For early Western practice it cites Tertullian's *De Baptismo* 7–8, AT 21, and Ambrose's *De Sacramentis* and *De Mysteriis*. But it nowhere cites Innocent I's letter to Decentius of Gubbio or the homily attributed to Faustus of Riez. It then refers generally to the very mixed liturgical witness of later Roman, Gallican, Romano-Gallican and Romano-Germanic liturgical materials, distinguishing them only in a bibliographical footnote.[10] It finally rests much of its case on later medieval documents of councils and popes " . . . which cast light on the importance of anointing while at the same time not allowing the laying on of hands to be obscured."[11] We note that *anointing* is emphasized over hand laying, despite what is recognized to be the liturgical tradition of the Latin Church, in which " . . . a laying of hands upon those to be confirmed was always prescribed before the anointing."[12]

The Apostolic Constitution then refers to Acts 8.15–17 in a context emphasizing hand laying, but without Innocent I's concern to link this through the apostles Peter and John to bishops alone. It also mentions Cyril of Jerusalem's explanation of the postbaptismal anointing as "the emblem of that wherewith Christ was anointed; and this is the Holy Spirit," an explanation which becomes, as we have seen, the formula for the postbaptismal chrismation by a presbyter in the eighth century Byzantine liturgy of baptism: "The seal of the gift of the Holy Spirit." From all this the document concludes that in both East and West . . .

"the most important place was occupied by the anointing, which in a certain way represents the apostolic laying on of hands. Since this anointing with chrism well represents the spiritual anointing of the Holy Spirit, who is given to the faithful, we intend to confirm its existence and importance."[13]

This is an extraordinary argument in view of the historical evidence it summarizes. Acts 8, to which Innocent I appealed, no less than the account of the first Pentecost in Acts 2, does not associate the giving of the Spirit with an anointing of any kind. Acts 8 associates it instead with apostolic hand laying. And the Eastern postbaptismal chrismation by a presbyter in its origin, like the one in AT 21 and that still in present Roman use, is christic and messianic rather than pneumatic. If one reads the whole context in which Cyril of Jerusalem explains the postbaptismal anointing it is clear that this same christic dimension prevails even there.[14] And as we have seen, the *Missale Gallicanum Vetus* and the *Bobbio Missal*,[15] no less than the *Stowe Missal*,[16] use as the formula of their *postbaptismal chrismation* words strongly redolent of the Verona AT 21 "Lord God" prayer, in which a bestowal of the Holy Spirit is not mentioned. Paul VI is correct in that "the most important place was occupied by the anointing"; but where the *anointing* holds that place in the later East, in Gaul, and indeed in Rome itself is in the *postbaptismal chrismation by a presbyter* rather than in consignation or confirmation by a bishop. Here the anointing is structurally a subordinate part of the bishop's hand laying, as AT 21 makes clear. And the Verona version of AT 21, as we have seen, does not associate a special bestowal of the Spirit with either gesture.

But the Apostolic Constitution, while not exactly ignoring such considerations, sweeps them aside:

"As regards the words which are pronounced in confirmation, we have examined with due consideration the dignity of the venerable formula used in the Latin Church, but we judge preferable the very ancient formula belonging to the Byzantine rite, by which the Gift of the Spirit which took place on the day of Pentecost is recalled (see Acts 2.1–4, 38). We therefore adopt this formula, rendering it almost word for word."[17]

The words are *Accipe Signaculum Doni Spiritus Sancti,* which are said as the forehead is anointed with chrism.

But what the above text is referring to in the Byzantine baptismal liturgy is not and never has been a rite of episcopal confirmation. It is the postbaptismal chrismation done by a presbyter, and it is not done with a hand laying. This same chrismation remains in the Roman baptismal liturgy, but is now to be omitted when adults and children of catechetical age are confirmed immediately after their baptism. This disposition increases the structural configuration of modern Roman confirmation to the Byzantine postbaptismal chrismation, and it is now done often by a presbyter, as is nearly always the case in Byzantine usage. The old Roman sequence of baptism and chrismation followed (even if years later) by episcopal confirmation remains only in the instance of infant baptism, where presbyters may not confirm except in danger of death. In these instances, however, bishops will eventually confirm such children by using the presbyteral postbaptismal chrismation formula taken from another tradition.

The matter and form of Roman confirmation have been Byzantinized, as has confirmation's place in the baptismal liturgy for adults and older children, and its usual minister, a presbyter. For those baptized and chrismated as infants, however, preconciliar practice if not preconciliar matter and form remains in force: confirmation must be celebrated by a bishop or a presbyter *delegated* by him, often after the candidates have already begun to receive communion. It might be argued that confirmation structurally has been given up in all but name in the case of adults and children of catechetical age, but is retained as a separate structure for those baptized as infants. This anomalous situation is the weakest aspect of the reform since it does not restore anything peculiarly Roman but creates something new on grounds that are liturgically syncretistic and may well turn out to be pastorally problematical.

The structure of the reformed rite of confirmation, at whatever time it takes place, will not be entirely unfamiliar to readers of this analysis. It takes place in four main steps.

1. The bishop or other celebrant, together with the presbyters who may be associated with him, lay or extend hands over the candidates.

2. The celebrant says the Gelasian redaction of AT's "Lord God" prayer, "All-powerful God."[18]

3. The celebrant, together with any associate presbyters, sign each candidate with chrism on the

forehead in the sign of the cross, saying "N., be sealed with the Gift of the Holy Spirit." No hand laying is mentioned in connection with this act.

4. Celebrant and confirmed exchange the words of Christian greeting, "The Lord be with you," "And also with you." No kiss is given.[19]

Several shifts are obvious here in view of the old *missa* rite in AT 21. First, the hand laying on individuals, or extension of hands over large groups, and the anointing are separated by the prayer rather than being done together after the prayer. Second, the prayer is an epiclesis expanded by listing the specific gifts of the Spirit. Third, the original consignation formula, which was trinitarian in AT and christic in Gelasian,[20] is now exclusively pneumatic in the manner of the Byzantine postbaptismal chrismation, as we have seen. Fourth, there is a greeting but no kiss. Fifth, the signation *in frontem* is not restricted to bishops but may also be done by presbyter-celebrants and associates. Thus the structural elements of prayer and hand laying together with episcopal ministry typical of the old *missa* are still present, but all are modified and given altered texts. The hand laying is de-emphasized and the signation with chrism *more byzantino* is emphasized.

But there is one other disposition to which we have already alluded and which deserves expanded comment. It is the stipulation in the *Rite of Christian Initiation of Adults* that when confirmation is celebrated immediately after baptism in the case of adults and children of catechetical age the postbaptismal chrismation by a presbyter is omitted.[21] This practice may render obsolete the old presbyteral chrismation after baptism in the Roman liturgy; but it leaves it, rather unaccountably as it seems, in place at the baptism of infants, when confirmation is not allowed to follow immediately. The reasons for this apparent anomaly may be that reformed confirmation, based structurally and theologically on the Byzantine postbaptismal chrismation, which is pneumatic, makes the Roman postbaptismal chrismation, which is christic and messianic,[22] redundant, confusing, or not as important as the pneumatic chrismation of confirmation.

In the baptismal tradition of East and West, however, the postbaptismal chrismation by a presbyter has been a far more widespread baptismal feature than the Roman peculiarity of a subsequent episcopal hand laying and second chrismation. The latter, as we have attempted to show, was rooted in the old non-pneumatic *missa* of AT 21, exported later to other Latin liturgical systems with accompanying changes and reinterpretations since the time of Innocent I at the beginning of the fifth century. As an episcopal ministry to the newly baptized and anointed in Christ as they began to celebrate their transformation amid the eucharistic fellowship where the Spirit flourishes, the old *missa* seems not to have regarded the postbaptismal chrismation as either redundant or confusing. Confusion and redundancy perhaps began to set in when the old *missa* was transmuted into a pneumatic act distinct from baptism, then separated from baptism and merged with disciplinary concerns, and finally put into competition with baptism as an educational sacrament said to confer a maturity that baptism did not.

Roman confirmation picked up a pneumatic character by the early fifth century. This remained linked to the *lauacrum regenerationis spiritus sancti* and its christic anointing, reiterating each time baptism and confirmation were celebrated as a unit the ancient doctrine according to which the Christ of God sends his life-giving Spirit, which in turn is the only authentic revealer of Jesus as Messiah-Christ. The eucharist of the newly baptized, chrismated, and consigned was then the first great celebration of this revelation's having taken root in people's lives. This is indicative of that necessary connection between the mission of the Son, which is to reveal the Father, and the mission of the Holy Spirit, who reveals Jesus to be the Anointed One of the Father. In the *joint* celebration of the initiatory sacraments this necessary connection is illustrated effectively as Son and Spirit come with the Father upon the baptized.[23] The neophytes are transformed only by the full action of no less than Spirit, Son, and Father.

There is no doubt that the entire initiatory reform was meant to restore this "joint celebration of the sacraments" for such fundamental theological reasons in the hope that the whole might affect Christian identity and pastoral practice for the better. The reform of confirmation, the most historically problematic and poorly understood of the three initiatory sacraments, was clearly meant to do at least two things. *First, it was meant to bring confirmation into a closer relationship to baptism.* Even the suppression of the postbaptismal chrismation, something regrettable on historical and theological grounds, now allows confirmation to follow baptism immediately as its pneumatic seal, "by water and Spirit." This is what necessitated the wide extension of opportunities for presbyters to confirm not merely by occasional delegation but by law. The extension must be seen not as a gesture of benevolence toward priests, or as a way of reducing the work load of bishops, but as a way of restoring confirmation *to baptism* despite the bishop's absence. This breaks an episcopal hegemony as minister of confirmation which extends all the way back to ancient *missa* practice which we have seen in AT 21 and other sources in the third century and afterwards.

Second, confirmation reform was meant to reiterate this sacrament's relationship to the eucharist, which consummates both baptism and confirmation. We have already noted this in terms of conciliar, liturgical, and canonical insistence that the authentic sequence of the sacraments of initiation is baptism-confirmation-eucharist. The matter may now be treated in terms of the canonical age for confirming those baptized in infancy.

b. The Question of Age
The question of the canonical age for confirming those baptized in infancy is governed by confirmation's relationship to eucharist. As confirmation is necessarily *subsequent* to baptism, it is no less necessarily *prior* to eucharist in the very grammar and logic of the three sacraments themselves.

Postponement of confirmation to a later age was urged upon the postconciliar *coetus* from many quarters for a variety of reasons, all of which were resisted in favor of the norm already recognized in tradition, the 1917 Code of Canon Law, and the ordinary papal magisterium.[24] This *ius vigens* set the age for confirmation of those baptized in infancy at the age of discretion, around the seventh year, and the same was reasserted in the *Rite of Confirmation* 11: "With regard to children, in the Latin Church the administration of confirmation is generally postponed until about the seventh year."[25] Canon 891 of the 1983 Code reiterates this but calls it "the age of discretion." The settlement on this age was not arbitrary, nor the result of reactionism, nor was it made out of ignorance about modern theories of personality development among the young. Rather, *it conformed to the usual time at which children were to begin receiving communion*, thus keeping intact the sequence of baptism-confirmation-eucharist. This was something the *coetus* under the direction of Bernard Botte determined to foster in addition to keeping confirmation as close to baptism as possible.

But pressure to create a loophole for postponing confirmation to a later age was too strong to be resisted entirely. The loophole was included in the *Rite of Confir-*

mation 11 and canon 891 as something which for pastoral reasons only episcopal conferences, not individual bishops, might permit. In such a case, the *Rite* cautions, " . . . the necessary precautions should be taken so that children will be confirmed at the proper time, even before the use of reason, where there is danger of death or other serious difficulty. They should not be deprived of the benefit of this sacrament."[26]

The minutes of the *coetus* and writings by its director and secretary criticize the delay of confirmation due to its being an alleged sacrament of maturity for adolescents and they emphasize the norm rather than the loophole.[27] This may be why canon 891 appears in 1983 to be somewhat stronger, perhaps, than the 1971 *Rite*, avoiding mention of "maturity" and specifying canonically only a decision of the entire regional episcopal conference, the judgment of the minister in view of a *grave* cause, or the danger of death as reasons for altering the normal age for receiving confirmation. This tightened up an earlier draft of the canon, which mentioned only the age "customary for the region."[28] Instead of loosening the discipline envisioned by the initiatory reforms as a whole when they were worked out in the late 1960's and early 1970's, the Code of 1983 stiffens it.

This is particularly clear when one reads canon 891 in context of canon 842:2, which sets the standard for the whole legal expression of the initiatory norm: "The sacraments of baptism, confirmation, and the Most Holy Eucharist so converge that they are required for full Christian initiation." This is a doctrinal statement from which specific laws will be drawn—for example canon 891 regarding the normative age for confirmation of those baptized in infancy. Canon 891 must therefore not be seen in isolation but must be interpreted in light of canon 842:2, just as the loophole section in the *Rite of Confirmation* 11 must be construed in view of the same paragraph's statement of the normal age. Should episcopal conferences undertake to designate some other age for confirmation it will be incumbent upon them to do so in such a way that the initiatory strategy of relating confirmation to baptism and consummating it in eucharist not be vitiated.[29] The paradigm for all this remains that found in the *Rite of Christian Initiation of Adults*, whose attitude on this matter is distilled in canon 866: "Unless a grave reason prevents it, an adult who is baptized is to be confirmed immediately after baptism and participate in the celebration of the Eucharist, also receiving communion." The same applies for children of catechetical age who request baptism.[30] When these norms are taken together with the *Rite of Confirmation* 11 and 13 and with canon 891, which require confirmation to be administered around age seven or the use of reason, it is "a sound and evident interpretation that confirmation should be conferred at First Eucharist."[31]

When one reads the documents reforming confirmation in relationship to the whole sweep of the Consilium's reform strategy for Christian initiation it becomes clear that the loophole allowing postponement of confirmation to later years (a practice which got its start from no other reason, according to Botte, than the unavailability of bishops during the middle ages)[32] sits in the initiatory reform as an awkward compromise out of which too much should not be made. The initiatory norm clearly points to full initiation of all who are deemed acceptable by baptism, the chrismation of confirmation, and first eucharistic communion. The loophole in the *Rite of Confirmation* 11 and canon 891, allowing a delay in celebrating confirmation for those baptized in infancy, represents a holdover of abnormal practice which came about as the result of compromises during later centuries when the liturgy and sacramental theology had sunk into vari-

ous states of disruption and decay. The delay of confirmation is anything but a modern step forward created
by new insights into personality development and educational methods. The delay preceded these insights
by centuries, only to be picked up and championed by
some therapists and educators quite recently in well-
meant attempts to give some rationale to a practice
which is patently abnormal. The initiatory reform of
the Council and Consilium has rather boldly undertaken to remove, or at least reduce significantly, abnor-
malities such as confirmation delayed so long after baptism that anticipating communion before confirmation
would have perforce to be regarded as both necessary
and normal.

Putting confirmation back into its initiatory context between baptism and first eucharist, which is the clearly
stated intent of the reforms, anchors confirmation
once again where it belongs as a modest rite of transi-
tion from Pool to Table. This strategy, in favor of
which deep liturgical tradition and theology both
speak strongly, could well free the Church to develop
more resilient catechetical programs and more appropriate rituals (perhaps of reconciliation to the Church)
which can better deal with the myriad stresses felt by
modern adolescents as they approach civil enfranchisement and roles of responsibility in the Church.

Allowing confirmation to continue to wander apart
from baptism and eucharist as its native frame of reference disrupts the entire initiatory norm and distracts
pastoral effort by seeming to suggest that initiation is
consummated not by eucharist but by episcopal confirmation and its gift of the Spirit, unaccountably de-
layed and separated from baptism by years and condi-
tioned on attaining some level of formal religious education. This inevitably magnifies confirmation at the ex-
pense of baptism in popular perception, seeming to
make both baptism and first communion (neither of

which require a special visit of the bishop) somehow less than confirmation.

The liturgical, sacramental, and theological inconveniences of such a perception come at a high price, despite short-term pastoral gains which may be alleged. These gains often turn out to be anomalous—as when confirmation, delayed well into adolescence and advertised as final and mature entrance into the Church, becomes in fact a rite of exit from it into ordinary secular life now free of ecclesiastical constraints. When this happens it is not difficult for young people to conclude that sacramental symbolism and its actual effects are two entirely different matters which cancel each other out.

3. ESTIMATES AND PROBLEMS

Throughout this analysis of confirmation's origins and reform it has become apparent that several problems continue to shadow this sacrament.

The first problem has been that of accumulated symbolism. There is a limit to the amount of symbolism a rite can support before the basic architecture of the rite itself begins to crumble.[33] Beginning straightforwardly as the dismissal of neophytes, by episcopal hand laying and prayer, from baptism and its chrismation into first eucharist, confirmation became first a distinct giving of the Spirit enhancing the unique centrality of apostolic ministry by anointing *in frontem* by the bishop. It later merged with Gallican concerns for episcopal oversight of baptism and was separated farther from baptism by the infrequency of episcopal presence. Medieval theologians found the sacrament in this condition, administered (if at all) in late childhood or adolescence, and assigned to it the supplying of graces which were either not given in baptism or given in only an inchoate way to infants. Maturity began to take on biological, personal, cultural, and civil emphases at this point, emphases which could be subsumed into the category of educational endeavor with the Renaissance and the invention of printing in the fifteenth century. In the sixteenth century, the Reformation churches either got rid of confirmation entirely or kept it as the conclusion of an educational process by which children learned the printed catechism. More recently Catholic no less than Protestant churches have expanded this educational dimension of confirmation with programs of youth therapy, and Catholics have attempted to integrate all this into formal school programs linking education to final sacramental incorporation into the Church.

The multiple symbolisms of washing, sealing, incorporation, death and resurrection always clustered around the central axis of the paschal mystery of Jesus the Christ. Keeping this focus clear was the purpose of patristic catechesis both before and after baptism. As such catechesis declined from the early middle ages onward, these initiatory symbolisms were exploited in new ways and for other purposes, giving rise to two clusters of initiatory symbolisms less and less in touch with each other—the baptismal and pneumatic clusters which resulted in the initiatory rite collapsing into two separate and distinct sacraments with separate and distinct effects. The collapse resulted in two separate and distinct classes of Christians. One was a proletariat of the merely baptized who, like the Samaritans of Acts 8, had not yet received the Spirit and were therefore excluded from the eucharist. The other was the confirmed, who would come to be finally compared with the ranks of the ordained by the quasi-ordination of episcopal prayer, hand laying, and anointing.[34] This cleavage in Church membership is one factor that has produced the perception of a category of "first-class citizenship" in the Church conferred only by ordination, to which all must have a right. It is clear that the symbolic perception of those who propose the ordination of women is not entirely inaccurate, given the effects of ritual collapse in the rites of Christian initiation due to the weight of accumulated symbolism forcing baptism and confirmation apart, and associating the latter with special status.

A second problem is the loss of symbolic intelligibility.[35] Symbols work by triggering whole chains of further associations. This is a function of the symbol's own intelligibility, and the symbol is intelligible to the extent that one who engages in it is able to relate it to elements in his or her own human experience. It is this human experience which is the context of intelligible discourse, and symbols normally play a large and fundamental part in any such discourse. What confirmation's "anointing with Spirit" relates to in one's own human experience has never been easy to say, and trying only to *say* it may be part of the problem. It may be that *saying* something about so experientially elusive a thing as "spirit" is not nearly so helpful as a touch in intimacy by someone whom one loves and respects, or an odor that is delightful and profoundly memorable like baking bread or the perfume of a friend. Tactile and olfactory experiences are as extremely powerful as they are elusive and difficult to put into words, not unlike the Spirit of God. One suspects that these experiences are what give one's bath or shower such a renewing effect on the psyche. This counsels that our attempts to verbalize what confirmation means should perhaps be less ideological and take the tactile and olfactory elements of the rite, especially as they relate fundamentally to the washing of baptism (a highly tactile experience) and the gustatory experience of communion, more seriously. We might learn more about the basic human experience which these overlooked ritual elements reveal, and this revelation in turn might plunge us into levels deeper than ideology toward what the whole of Christian initiation can reveal to us of the God who redeems us in his Christ. But a few drops of water, extended hands which do not touch, and a dab of odorless oil are not strong enough to trigger many further associations, especially when these pallid acts are overwhelmed by talk as they are done. No liturgy is merely a notional thing about which we may do little more than talk. The talk will mean far less than it should if the elemental sensory aspects of a rite are reduced to a minimum and the experiences of these are distrusted or misunderstood. Such a thing brings rite itself under suspicion and re-enforces experiential no less than symbolic illiteracy, destroying the tactile, aesthetic, and symbolic forces which make the very need for words necessary. The results are prolix liturgy, catechesis which is top-heavy with conceptual content, and a perception among many that to be a first-class Christian one must have a degree in theology, re-enforcing that cleavage in Church membership already mentioned.

A third problem may be a misunderstanding of the connection between memorial (anamnesis) *and invocation* (epiclesis) *in worship.*[36] If baptism, for example, is understood as little more than a liturgical mime of the historical event of Jesus' baptism by John in the Jordan, designed to aid the faithful in remembering Jesus as he was, then it stands in need of an invocation which calls on God to provide the Holy Spirit to vivify what would otherwise remain dead narration and pious but powerless remembering. But neither baptism nor eucharist are devices for remembering historical events in order to set up contexts of piety within which God's power may be called on to act. The eucharist is not a mime of the Last Supper, but the Church's Spirit-filled thanksgiving for all God has wrought, and which the Spirit reveals in Christ for human salvation. Similarly, baptism is not a mime of the

Jordan event, but the Spirit-revealed beginning of our reconciliation to God in Christ, the Church's *lauacrum regenerationis spiritus sancti.*

Put crudely, baptism does not wait to work until the invocation of the Holy Spirit at confirmation is added to it. For memorial and invocation, *anamnesis* and *epiclesis,* are in reality one, since the deepest memory of God is made possible only when the Holy Spirit reveals Jesus to be the Christ of God. To remember Jesus in any other way is not essentially different from remembering Rutherford B. Hayes. The Spirit is invoked over baptism's waters, at the eucharistic table, and in the ordination of major ministers not to vivify the dead recital of past deeds, or to bring them somehow into a present from which they are otherwise absent. Rather, the Spirit is invoked to proclaim and exhibit God as *always* present and active in the faithful assembly's life and memory. *Anamnesis* and *epiclesis* are therefore complementary and inseparable, the inside and outside of a single reality, the reality of God's Word become flesh, the reality of Christ's broken body becoming a Body corporate, the reality of his baptism into messiahship and unto death becoming a People of faith and of a Spirit who teaches them all these things. In baptism the Spirit discloses Jesus' messianic identity and present ministry to those who remember in faith; the Spirit is not there to remedy baptism's shortcomings or to complete its unfinished business in confirmation. Viewing memory and invocation otherwise gives us a view of the Holy Spirit as being absent from baptism and operating without subordination to it—a view which ultimately sustains not only two distinct initiatory policies for infants and adults but, alas, a cloven membership in that Assembly of faithful assemblies, the Church.[37]

The recent reforms of initiation generally, and of confirmation in particular, provide a firm basis upon which problems such as these, which run very deep and are not susceptible to single or easy solutions, may be dealt with. The reform of confirmation had to be a very radical one, given the state of confusion over this sacrament as it had changed during the course of its history, and given its central position in the traditional initiatory sequence of baptism-confirmation-eucharist, as we have seen. The Apostolic Constitution of Paul VI which introduced the *Rite of Confirmation* in 1971 puts the sacrament in a strongly baptismal context which counsels that it be celebrated earlier rather than later for those who were baptized in infancy. The Apostolic Constitution also changes the liturgical structure on which the rite is based from the old episcopal *missa* structure of AT 21, which was pneumaticized by the time of Innocent I, to one based on the Byzantine postbaptismal chrismation by a presbyter. This shift has the logical effect of diminishing the old Roman postbaptismal chrismation by a presbyter and of alleviating in law the centuries-old hegemony bishops had in administering confirmation, thus moving confirmation even more closely to baptism. The historic connection of confirmation with baptism is thus more clearly evident today than at any time perhaps since the early middle ages, even though theology and religious educators seem not yet to have grasped this vision. This is not surprising since it is far easier to change the liturgy than to change deeply set attitudes people bring to the liturgy.

There can be no doubt that the Apostolic Constitution and the *Rite of Confirmation* have done their best to fulfill the conciliar mandate that "The rite of Confirmation is to be revised and the intimate connection which this sacrament has with the whole of Christian initiation is to be more clearly set forth" (CL 71). But the conditions under which the rite is to be done create counter thrusts and new ambiguities when they emphasize different procedures for those baptized as adults and children of catechetical age on the one hand, and for those baptized as infants on the other. The former are baptized, confirmed, and communicated in the same service, even by a presbyter in the bishop's absence. The latter are baptized and chrismated as infants and then confirmed by a bishop years later (around the seventh year according to law, even later in various places). The theological question of why, given the almost exclusive emphasis on giving the gift of the Holy Spirit in confirmation, the Spirit is withheld from certain of the baptized but not from others on the basis of age is left unanswered. Should one try to answer the question by citing the need for catechesis in preparation for receiving the Holy Spirit in confirmation, someone else might then ask why such catechesis is not therefore even more necessary for baptism. Unless one delays baptism it seems that the catechetical answer loses force. Such a delay is not in sight.

But the issue is even more extensive. The difference in procedure for the two different age groups requires what are in fact two quite different catecheses of confirmation which must conform themselves to the widely different contexts in which one and the same sacramental act is experienced. Nor can it be ruled out that these different contexts and catecheses may eventually force the evolution of two different "sacraments" of confirmation: one that is strongly baptismal and transformational, and one that is just as strongly educational, therapeutic, and prophylactic. As this happens the equivocations which have shadowed this sacrament since the time when Innocent I's consignation began to merge with Gallican confirmation will not vanish but merely take on a new aspect which will result in two very different liturgical contexts of initiation, as one can see in these two sequences:

I *Baptismal-transformational*	II *Educational-prophylactic*
	Baptism-chrismation in infancy
Pre-evangelization Evangelization Catechumenate	Schooling Catechetical-educational programs *Penance* *First Communion* Catechetical-educational programs
Baptism *Confirmation* (presbyter) *Eucharist, First Communion*	*Confirmation* (bishop)

Children and adults coming to confirmation in Sequence I have a proximate experience of conversion and baptism, and can look forward to their first communion. Children and adolescents coming to confirmation in Sequence II have no personal memory of their own baptism and in many cases have already been receiving communion for some time since their first confession. The perceptions of each group of confirmands are thus very different, both sacramentally and psychologically, and require different catecheses tailored to what happens to them in two different initiatory sequences and liturgical contexts. Sequence I culminates in the *seal of the eucharist.* Sequence II culminates in the *seal of confirmation* enhanced by the bishop's presence, the eucharist having already been anticipated. This is symptomatic of functionally different, even divergent, theologies of Christian identity which are imbedded in each sequence, something which the Council's reintegration purposes were at pains to resolve.

In Sequence I, for example, the Holy Spirit is pre-
sumed to be at work throughout, beginning with its
pentecostal impulse upon the Church to proclaim the
Gospel and to deal reverently and responsibly with
the conversions to faith which God's grace causes. The
Spirit remains at work in the discernment which cate-
chists, pastors, and the faithful must exercise as catechumens strive to conform their lives to the burgeon-
ing grace of faith. In this sequence it is regrettable that
the messianic chrismation after baptism has been omitted. This traditionally provided a cornerstone upon
which to base a perception of the Anointed One who
gives the Spirit so that we may know him as the
Christ of God. The weakness of a vigorous theology
and piety of the Holy Spirit in the Western churches,
so often lamented, might have been strengthened by a
renewed perception of this relationship between
Messiah-Christ and Holy Spirit.

In Sequence II, on the other hand, the Holy Spirit may
be seen at work more indirectly in the faith of parents
who offer their offspring for baptism-chrismation in infancy, and who sacrifice to send them later to school
and enroll them in programs of religious education.
Confirmation in connection with these programs, and
administered at some time during the candidates' primary or secondary schooling, puts the gift of the Spirit
in a context which inevitably interprets the sacrament
less in terms of a transforming conversion and initiation into eucharistic and ecclesial fellowship than of
education and solving adolescent personality problems
consequent upon puberty and entry into civil society.
Sacramental initiatory sequence is subordinated to
these latter purposes and undergoes an implicit reinterpretation which is at variance with that embodied in
Sequence I. Therapeutic penance for sins, committed
or not, is thus seen to be somehow requisite for first
communion although the seal of the gift of the Holy

Spirit is not. This illustrates the pneumatological weakness already mentioned.

The theology embedded in the old *missa* of AT 21 might have handled this well enough by saying that it is in baptism itself that one is bathed and regenerated by the Holy Spirit, and that this is precisely what makes eucharist possible as the Church's premier Spirit-filled event. But Innocent I shifted the giving of the Spirit to the old *missa's* signation with chrism *in frontem,* in effect "depneumaticizing" baptism (as Jerome seems to have recognized). When this consignation was removed even farther from baptism as it merged with Gallican confirmation, the stage was set for conditions other than baptism to determine when the Holy Spirit will be conferred and eucharistic communion may begin. These conditions today are often employed in effect to coerce a required amount of exposure to catechetical and educational programs. Although one regrets to say it, this coercion may be one factor which leads many young people to regard confirmation as the special event which marks their "graduation" from ecclesiastical constraint into the apparent freedoms of secular life. While education and therapy doubtless need to be done, these endeavors must not be allowed to reinterpret sacraments and alter their integrated liturgical sequence to the extent that sacraments and liturgy become unintelligible apart from such educational and therapeutic endeavors.

One way to help keep this situation from becoming worse might be to take more seriously the thrust of the reform, linking confirmation in all instances as closely to baptism as possible and never allowing first communion to precede it. Following the logic of its Byzantinization as *the* postbaptismal chrismation, linking confirmation always to baptism might require its being done for the most part by presbyters, even by delegation, unless the bishop can be present to preside over the whole liturgy of initiation. A firm insistence on this discipline over time by episcopal conferences would be within the bounds of current law and obedient to the clear intent of the reform itself, which gives no priority to those educational and therapeutic dimensions which have clustered around this sacrament in recent years and counselled its delay. More importantly, however, such a firm and consistent discipline would allow confirmation to speak for itself once again amid the welter of conflicting opinions about what it is or ought to be. Over time it might then become possible for people to hear what confirmation has to say, namely, that baptism and eucharist are the premier sacraments of Christian initiation and confirmation itself nothing more nor less than the Roman Catholic Church's way of linking the two.

After being brought to full sacramental initiation in the Church no later than the age of reason, subsequent catechesis of those baptized in infancy would then be free to focus not on confirmation but on their assuming an increasingly knowledgeable public capacity in the Church sometime between the age of reason and young adulthood. Such a procedure could culminate in a liturgy of reconciliation to the Church (if needed) and a solemnization of holy communion. The catechetical focus would then be where it ought to be: on the eucharist as the sacrament of Christian maturity par excellence.[38] Sacramental sequence is thus kept intact and the educational and therapeutic needs of the young are free of having to be seen always in terms of confirmation. If it is decided that the Church's ministry to its youth needs formal celebrations of puberty, of the reception of one's driver's license, of graduation from programs of religious education, of spiritual awakening, and of civil majority, then paraliturgical rites to fill such needs can be developed without having to make confirmation cover them all,

111

to the confusion of many. Votive masses, Bible services, *Te Deums,* marriage, penance, and solemnized communion are all strictly liturgical options for such needs as well. Why confirmation must substitute for all these is a question which finally has no compelling answer.

Some might suggest that confirmation be abolished altogether as a confusing mistake or in the interests of ecumenical rapprochement since it is sustained, as we have seen, in no other historic liturgical system but the Roman. This point is not ill taken, but it is historically naive. Confirmation has been around in Roman initiatory polity in one form or another since at least the beginning of the fifth century, if not the third, and something that old is in possession of nine points of sacramental and liturgical law, so to speak. American Episcopalians tried to suppress confirmation in their 1979 *Book of Common Prayer* and not only failed but added to the confusion over its nature and use by bishops apart from baptism.[39]

Still others might point out that the logical conclusion of the Roman reform of confirmation, bringing it back into an intimate connection with baptism and basing it on the Byzantine postbaptismal chrismation, would seem to be to perform the rite on every occasion when baptism is conferred, even upon infants. Those who are initiated in infancy by baptism and confirmation would then, like everyone else, be given first communion, even if under the species of wine alone for infants, in order to seal the completeness and integrity of their initiation into the ecclesial fellowship, where the Spirit flourishes. The Roman Church continued to do this through the twelfth century and the various Eastern Churches, Catholic as well as Orthodox, still do this today. The point is not without merit and has both precedent and current Eastern practice on its side. Should episcopal conferences undertake to enforce firmly the discipline of reformed initiatory policy as contained in the present liturgical books and in canon law it may be that, over time, moving in this traditional direction could become a reasonable option. One doubts that this is presently the case, but the door to such a possibility should consciously be kept open.

Steps must be taken one at a time because the liturgy in its healthiest state grows by evolution rather than revolution, keeping its participants with it rather than alienating them from it. The Roman Catholic Church today, thanks to the Second Vatican Council and its post-conciliar Consilium, possesses a better integrated and restored initiation policy which, if firmly enforced and given a chance to work according to the vision which brought it into being, can provide solid ground for resolving liturgical, theological, and pastoral anomalies which confuse and enervate. This policy was worked out by pastors no less than scholars who were deeply aware that good practice does not proceed from bad theology, and that good theology and good practice are both essential for the Church in carrying out its mission. Initiatory matters stand at the heart of both because they involve the constant genesis of the Church as a communon of shared faith in every generation. Baptism is the way the Church begins; eucharist is the way the Church lives, sanctified and sanctifying for the life of the world. The Church's restored initiatory policy clearly lifts up the eucharist, attained through baptism and confirmation, as the supreme icon of how the Church goes about this ministry in the world—praying to God through Christ for that world and giving thanks for it to its Creator by its Redeemer in the Holy Spirit who reveals it for what it is by the hand of the one and the blood of the other. Made possible by baptism and confirmation, the eucharist is nothing other than the Church in the world alive at its deepest and most mysterious level, celebrating its fertile nuptials with its divine source. Any other ecclesiology is no more than a partial anecdote about this reality which is of God.

The eucharist is not merely a metaphor about the Church. The eucharist is the basic analogy which reproduces the contour of divine purpose in the Christ of God for the world, a purpose into the very center of which the Holy Spirit sweeps the Church by grace, faith, and sacrament. The eucharist evangelizes its participants each time it is celebrated with the good news that they are the Church, Christ's Body, that the Church is no less a mystery than are their own lives of chosenness in faith, and that all they are and do culminates in God's Christ, who has given into their hearts his first and final gift of life-giving Spirit. That Spirit calls them in peace to this Table and is invoked there as "confirmation of their faith in truth."[40]

This is why all sacraments, especially the other two sacraments of initiation, baptism and confirmation, are ordered to the eucharist as their consummation. It is also why in the churches of an earlier day it occurred to no one to baptize even an infant without also chrismating, consigning or confirming (in the West), and communicating the initiate. As infants (a word used for all the newly baptized, regardless of age) needed physical food, so also they needed spiritual food to grow into full and active possession of their faith. As baptized Christians they were thought to have even more need of that supreme sacrament of the communion into which they had been admitted by the bath of regeneration of the Holy Spirit than anyone else. Catechesis was provided them, especially if they had been initiated in infancy, as they became capable of it; this happened less in an organized programmatic way than in a holistic manner through the extended family and their increasingly complex interactions with a Christian culture. The style of faith thus evoked in them was not so much clear-cut and notional, by modern standards, as it was what we today might characterize as folkloric. But it ran deep, surviving despite the slow dissolution of the old initiatory policy which had given it birth. It was in fact tough enough to endure in many places, often with astonishing power, into the modern age even in hostile environments such as Soviet Russia and Ethiopia. Of such faith one cannot say, in the words of John Donne, "Tis all in peeces, all cohaerence gone."

Whatever else may be said about such a folkloric style of faith one should remember that it is based not on *no* catechesis but on a type of catechesis which has little in common with what we regard as catechesis today. This latter is the product of recent educational techniques which carry a strong emphasis not on groups such as the extended family and the culture but on individual autonomy. When absorbed by catechesis, these modern educational techniques can make faith seem less a corporate possession liturgically celebrated than something one must put together for oneself with professional help out of an array of options distilled and presented by academic theology. This may tend to atomize faith into a set of problems and issues which are presented with little or no context to minds which over time become worn down and bemused by the sheer weight of information required for making decisions. Such minds will finally find little time for sacraments and lose their ability to follow the essentially humane and analogical way in which sacraments speak.

Sacraments always speak in a particular context and provide perspective and orientation within that context. Like their participants, sacraments are rooted always in a present which is aware of its past not as an impersonal, rigorously objective, and statistical chronology, but as story. Story chooses from the welter of facts certain events of importance in the cultural memory and then raises these to the level of analogies for the present. Such analogies are not idle. Without them we are hard put to frame ourselves as social beings who are what we are as the result of interactions between those who have preceded us and between our own selves and our contemporaries. Rooting us into the soil of a common story, these analogies do for us roughly what instinct does for animals: they help us survive by telling us in myriad ways, not all of which are purely notional, who we are in relation to all else. They provide us with parables of normality in the present from which we may distil norms for the future. This is why analogies are neither infallible nor static. Subsequent generations must reformulate them constantly in light of unforseeable new circumstances, an endeavor which takes the courage to run risks and is the main business of any vital culture as it moves through time. The constant reformulation of the culture's story and the analogies of normality it affords may never regard the past as anything less than a tutor for the present which enables a reasonable future. This is why tradition, another name for a culture's main business, is never merely about past things but about the present within which a future is always begotten.

Baptism and eucharist are the main analogies produced by the Christian story from the beginning, and confirmation is another analogy which the Roman Church's particular story has produced in order, as we have seen, to transact the relationship between them. No less than any other culture, the Church must pay closest attention to how its sacramental analogies are reformulated within the present for the future's sake, for the matter of perennial concern in all cultures is that of survival. This book has attempted to learn from the past in order to be better informed in the present how the sacramental analogy of confirmation works in exerting influence on baptism and eucharist, and how these two in turn hold confirmation in being. It is clear that the authentic intelligibility of the Roman Church's three initiatory sacramental analogies is only to be fully ascertained in their close complementarity and sequence. So long as confirmation exists it stands to warp and damage seriously our perception of baptism and eucharist if we allow it to wander and give equivocal witness to the nature not only of Christian initiation but of Christian identity in the Church and world as well.

The origins of confirmation suggest that it began, at the latest by the end of the second or beginning of the third century, in Rome as a more than ordinarily solemn episcopal *missa* of neophytes from their baptism into their first eucharist without any reference to their receiving the Holy Spirit at this point in the initiatory sequence. One concludes from this that confirmation should not be made too much over; it is certainly not to be understood as being on the same level with the premier New Testament rites of baptism and eucharist, even less as in competition with either of these. Making too much over confirmation by forcing it to bear more symbolism than its fundamentally modest structure and subordinate position between baptism and eucharist can support is perhaps one reason for confusion over what it is and does.

One thing it cannot possibly do is to supply a Holy Spirit who was somehow absent from baptism—as though the Holy Spirit were alien to the baptized until they are confirmed. Another thing confirmation cannot do is "ordain" the laity, for confirmation is not a ministerial but an initiatory sacrament. And one doubts that confirmation in all its structural modesty is, in the regular course of things, able or meant to accomplish all the educational, therapeutic, and pro-phylactic effects claimed for it by religious educators and others. Nor does confirmation constitute the gift of "Christian community," which originates solely in the *lauacrum regenerationis spiritus sancti* and is consummated solely in the eucharist. How confirmation strengthens the baptized in some way different from the eucharist, or more or less specifically than the other sacraments, or how it increases baptismal grace by the gift of the Holy Spirit who is already present and active in baptism are questions that theologians have been arguing about for centuries, with no end in sight.

These are problems. But a problem far greater than any of these would be to ignore the liberating thrust of confirmation's recent reform in a richer and larger context as one part of Christian initiation framed by baptism before and eucharist after. This reform, para-doxically and no doubt unintentionally, ends by taking a position not entirely dissimilar from that to which our structural analysis of confirmation's origins has led us, namely, that confirmation as we have come to know it is not found at the fountainhead of Roman initiatory practice in the Verona text of AT 21. What we found there instead was an early non-pneumatic episcopal *missa*. What the reform of 1971 did in struc-tural terms, at least, was to do away with confirmation in all but name, turning it into a postbaptismal chrismation using a pneumatic Byzantine formula and de-emphasizing both the hand laying and exclusively episcopal ministry. The purpose of this quite radical reform was clearly to bring confirmation into a more intimate relationship with baptism once more, the ven-erable usage of the Latin Church notwithstanding.

Thus it is that confirmation, which began in one liturgi-cal structure, seems to have come to an end in yet another, its history moving tortuously from *missa* to a postbaptismal chrismation. This is the way the mandate of the Council has been achieved: "The rite of Confirmation is to be revised and the intimate connection which this sacrament has with the whole of Christian initiation is to be more clearly set forth" (CL 71).

NOTES

All quotations of the 1983 Code of Canon Law are from *Code of Canon Law: Latin-English Edition* (Canon Law Society of America, Washington 1983).

1. Coetus a studiis 22, *Relatio qua describitur futurus ritus baptismi adultorum*, schemata n. 77, De Rituali 2, April 1965; in Michael J. Balhoff, "Age for Confirmation: Canonical Evidence," *The Jurist* 45:2 (1985) 549–587, especially 558; also his larger study, *The Legal Interrelatedness of the Sacraments of Initiation: New Canonical Developments in the Latin Rite from Vatican II to the New Code of Canon Law* (Washington 1984).

2. *The Rites of the Catholic Church* (= *The Rites*) 30, emphasis added.

3. *The Rites* 321.

4. This echoes the *Rite of Christian Initiation of Adults* 34, quoted above.

5. *The Rites* 322-323; canon 866. This implies that baptized infants who are confirmed in danger of death (canon 891) should then be communicated.

6. For background see J.D.C. Fisher, *Baptism in the Medieval West* (London 1965); Nathan Mitchell, "Dissolution of the Rite of Christian Initiation," *Made, Not Born*, 50–82.

7. *Rite of Christian Initiation of Adults* 34–35, 223; *The Rites* 30, 101.

8. *RCIA* 46, 228; *The Rites* 34, 103.

9. *Acta Apostolicae Sedis* 63 (1971) 657–664; *The Rites* 310–317.

10. *The Rites* 313, note 12.

11. *The Rites* 313.

12. *The Rites* 314–315.

13. *The Rites* 315.

14. Mystagogical Catechesis 3 (on 1 John 2.20–28); Whitaker 26–27.

15. See Chapter Two, note 31.

16. Whitaker 202: "You pour chrism over his brow, saying, 'May God the Father of our Lord Jesus Christ, who hath regenerated thee by water and the Holy Spirit, and who hath given thee remission of sins through the laver of regeneration and of blood, himself anoint thee with his holy chrism unto eternal life.' "

17. *The Rites* 315. Paradoxically, the "very ancient formula belonging to the Byzantine rite" is probably not older than one in the *Gelasian Sacramentary* (eighth century reflecting older usage, probably of the sixth), which reads: "The sign of Christ unto life eternal"; Whitaker 178. A certain modern prejudice in favor of Byzantine antiquity and clarity is evident in the Apostolic Constitution, as it is in recent ecumenical work on baptism. See Cyrille Argenti, "Chrismation" in *Ecumenical Perspectives on Baptism, Eucharist and Ministry*, M. Thurian,et.al.(Faith and Order Paper 116, Geneva 1983) 46–47; rightly criticized by B. Spinks, "Vivid Signs of the Spirit? The Lima Text on Baptism and Some Recent English Language Baptismal Liturgies," *Worship* 60 (1986) 232–246, especially 238.

18. RCIA 269; *The Rites* 115–116. Rite of Confirmation 25; *The Rites* 329.

19. RCIA 270; *The Rites* 116. Rite of Confirmation 26–28; *The Rites* 329–330.

20. AT 21: "I anoint you with holy oil in God the Father almighty and Christ Jesus and the holy Spirit"; Cuming 20. *Gelasian:* "The sign of Christ unto life eternal"; Whitaker 178, 186. Interestingly, *Ordo Romanus XI*, a baptismal order slightly later than Gelasian but witnessing to the same rite,

gives as the signation formula: "In the Name of the Father and of the Son and of the Holy Ghost;" Whitaker 194.

21. RCIA 35, 224; *The Rites* 30, 101.

22. E.g. AT 21; Cuming 20. Ambrose *De Mysteriis* 29–30; Whitaker 122. *Gelasian Sacramentary XLIV*. 94; Whitaker 178. The present formula, based on *Gelasian*, is in RCIA 224; *The Rites* 101: "God, the Father of our Lord Jesus Christ, has freed you from all sin, given you a new birth by water and the Holy Spirit, and welcomed you into his holy people. He now anoints you with the chrism of salvation. As Christ was anointed Priest, Prophet, and King, so may you live always as a member of his body, sharing everlasting life. Amen." Chrismation on the crown of the head then follows in silence.

23. RCIA 34; *The Rites* 30.

24. E.g., canon 788 of the 1917 Code and the encyclical *Abrogata* of Leo XIII in 1897 defending the right of the young to confirmation.

25. *The Rites* 321.

26. *The Rites* 322. Although not stated explicitly, the caution would seem to imply that communion should be administered even to children who are confirmed before the usual age "where there is danger of death or other serious difficulty," as we have noted.

27. E.g., B. Botte, "Problèmes de la confirmation," *Questions liturgiques* 53 (1972) 5–6, reflecting earlier views in "A propos de la confirmation," *Nouvelle revue théologique* 88 (1966) 848–852; B. Kleinheyer, "Le nouveau rituel de la confirmation," *La Maison-Dieu* 110 (1972) 51–71. See Balhoff, *art. cit.* 562–566.

28. See Balhoff 569.

29. The 1972 decision of the United States episcopal conference, reiterated in 1984, to allow bishops of dioceses to determine individually what the age for confirmation is to be in their own jurisdictions thus appears to violate the spirit and letter of canon 891. And where an individual decision has the effect of putting reception of confirmation *after* first recep-

tion of holy communion there appears to be an ignoring of the doctrine expressed in canon 842:2. See Balhoff 580–582.

30. RCIA 46, 344; *The Rites* 34, 143.

31. Balhoff 574.

32. B. Botte, "A propos de la confirmation," 848–852.

33. N. Mitchell, "Dissolution of the Rite of Christian Initiation," 71–72.

34. The idea of confirmation as the "ordination of the laity" is something I notice in the *Shape of Baptism* 81–86.

35. Mitchell, 72–73.

36. Mitchell, 73–75.

37. I develop these points in"Symbolic Implications of Christian Initiation in Roman Catholicism Since the Second Vatican Council," *I Simboli dell' Iniziazione Cristiana* (Studia Anselmiana 87, Rome 1983) 223–241.

38. This was insisted upon by all the initiatory *coetus*, as we have seen.

39. See G. Austin, *Anointing with the Spirit* (New York 1985) 65–81. In the 1979 *Book of Common Prayer* baptism is concluded by a prayer and signation on the forehead (chrism is optional) with the words, "N., you are sealed by the Holy Spirit in Baptism and marked as Christ's own for ever. Amen." The rite is not called confirmation and is regularly done by a presbyter unless a bishop happens to be present. As such, the rite somewhat resembles that enacted by Paul VI in 1971, moving away from the old *missa* pattern of episcopal prayer and hand laying toward a Byzantine-like chrismation concluding baptism. Confirmation by bishops in the 1979 *Book of Common Prayer*, on the other hand, keeps the old *missa* pattern but relates it to post-initiatory concerns such as the renewal of baptismal promises. For this reason the rite can apparently be administered repeatedly to the same recipient since it no longer shares in baptism's once-for-all character.

40. AT 4; Cuming 11.

Bibliography

Andrieu, M, *Le Pontifical romain au moyen-âge*, 4 vols. (Vatican City, 1938–1941).

Argenti, Cyrille, "Chrismation," *Ecumenical Perspectives on Baptism, Eucharist and Ministry*, M. Thurian, ed. (Faith and Order Paper 116, Geneva 1983) 46–67.

Austin, Gerard, *Anointing with the Spirit. The Rite of Confirmation: The Use of Oil and Chrism* (New York 1985).

Balhoff, Michael J., "Age for Confirmation: Canonical Evidence," *The Jurist* 45:2 (1985) 549–587.

———. *The Legal Interrelatedness of the Sacraments of Initiation: New Canonical Developments in the Latin Rite from Vatican II to the New Code of Canon Law* (Washington 1984).

Bhaldraithe, E. de, "Problems of the Monastic Conventual Mass," *The Downside Review* 90 (1972) 169–182.

Borella, P., "La 'missa' o 'dimissio catechumenorum' nelle liturgia occidentali," *Ephemerides Liturgicae* 53 (1939) 60–110.

Botte, B., "Apropos de la confirmation," *Nouvelle revue theologique* 88 (1966) 848–852.

———. *La Tradition Apostolique de saint Hippolyte: essai de reconstitution* (LQF 39, Münster 1963).

———. "Problèmes de la confirmation," *Questions liturgiques* 53 (1972) 3–8.

Code of Canon Law: Latin-English Edition (Canon Law Society of America, Washington 1983).

Cuming, G.J., *Hippolytus: A Text for Students* (Bramcote 1976).

Dallen, James, *The Reconciling Community: The Rite of Penance* (New York 1986).

Dix, Gregory, *The Apostolic Tradition of St. Hippolytus of Rome* (London ²1968).

Documents of the Baptismal Liturgy. E.C. Whitaker, ed. (London 1960).

Dölger, F.J., *Antike und Christentum* 4 (1934) 95–137.

Duchesne, L., *Origines du culte chrétiene* [1899] (Paris 1925).

Easton, Burton Scott. *The Apostolic Tradition of Hippolytus* (Cambridge 1934).

Fisher, J.D.C., *Baptism in the Medieval West* (London 1965).

———. *Confirmation Then and Now* (London 1978).

Funk, F.X., *Didascalia et Constitutiones Apostolorum* (Paderborn 1905).

Gamber, K., *Missa Romensis* (Studia patristica et liturgica 3, Regensburg 1970).

———. *Ordo Antiquus Gallicanus. Der gallikanische Messritus des 6. Jahrhunderts* (Regensburg 1965).

Heinemann, Joseph, *Prayer in the Talmud: Forms and Patterns* (Studia Judaica 9, Berlin and New York 1977).

Itinerarium Egeriae. Editio Critica, A. Franceschini and R. Weber, eds. (CCL 175, Brepols-Turnholt 1958).

Jungmann, J.A., *Die lateinischen Bussriten in ihrer geschictlichen Entwicklung* (Innsbruck 1932).

———. *Gewordene Liturgie* (Innsbruck 1941).

———. *The Mass of the Roman Rite*, 2 vols. (New York 1951 and 1955).

Kavanagh, Aidan, "Confirmation: A Suggestion from Structure," *Worship* 58 (1984) 386–395.

———. *On Liturgical Theology* (New York 1985).

———. *The Shape of Baptism: The Rite of Christian Initiation* (New York 1978).

————. "Symbolic Implications of Christian Initiation in Roman Catholicism since the Second Vatican Council," *I Simboli dell' Iniziazione Cristiana* (Studia Anselmiana 87, Rome 1983) 223–241.

Kelly, J.N.D., *Jerome: His Life, Writings, and Controversies* (New York 1975).

Kilmartin, Edward, "Early African Legislation concerning Liturgical Prayer," *Ephemerides Liturgicae* 99 (1985) 105–127.

Kleinheyer, B., "Le nouveau rituel de la confirmation," *La Maison-Dieu* 110 (1972) 51–71.

Linderbauer, B., *S. Benedicti Regula Monachorum* (Mettern 1922).

Liturgies Eastern and Western, F.E. Brightman, ed. (Oxford 1896).

The Liturgy of the Eighth Book of 'The Apostolic Constitutions' Commonly Called the Clementine Liturgy, R.H. Cresswell, trans. and ed. (London 1924).

Krautheimer, Richard, *Rome: Profile of a City* (Princeton 1980).

Lampe, G.W.H., *The Seal of the Spirit* (London ²1967).

Marsh, Thomas, *Gift of Community: Baptism and Confirmation* Wilmington 1984).

Mathews, Thomas, *The Early Churches of Constantinople: Architecture and Liturgy* (University Park, PA 1971).

McCann, J. *The Rule of St. Benedict* (London 1952).

Mitchell, Leonel L., *Baptismal Anointing* (London 1966).

Mitchell, Nathan, "Dissolution of the Rite of Christian Initiation," *Made, Not Born: New Perspectives on Christian Initiation and the Catechumenate* (Notre Dame 1976) 50–82.

Mohrmann, Christine, "Missa," *Vigiliae Christianae* 12 (1958) 67–92.

Pinell, Jordi, "El oficio hispano-visigotico," *Hispania Sacra* 10 (1957) 385–427.

Quinn, Frank C., "Confirmation Reconsidered: Rite and Meaning," *Worship* 59 (1985) 354–369.

RB 1980: The Rule of St. Benedict, T. Fry et al., eds. (Collegeville 1980).

The Rites of the Catholic Church, vol. 1 (New York 1976, 1983).

Rituale Armenorum, F.C. Conybeare and A.J. Maclean, eds. (Oxford 1905).

The Rule of the Master, L. Eberle and C. Philippi, eds. (Kalamazoo 1977).

A Select Library of Nicene and Post-Nicene Fathers of the Christian Church, Philip Schaff and Henry Wace, eds., vol. 15 [1899] (Eerdmans Reprint, Grand Rapids n.d.).

Spinks, Brian, "Vivid Signs of the Spirit? The Lima Text on Baptism and Some Recent English Language Baptismal Liturgies," *Worship* 60 (1986) 232–246.

Steidle, B., "Commentationes in Regulam S. Benedicti," *Studia Anselmiana* 42 (1957).

———. *The Rule of St. Benedict* (Canon City 1967).

Taft, Robert, *Beyond East and West: Problems in Liturgical Understanding* (Washington 1984).

———. *The Great Entrance: A History of the Transfer of the Gifts and other Preanaphoral Rites of the Liturgy of St. John Chrysostom* (OCA 200, Rome 1975).

———. "The Inclination Prayer before Communion in the Byzantine Liturgy of St. John Chrysostom: A Study in Comparative Liturgy," *Ecclesia Orans* 3:1 (1986) 29–60.

———. "The Liturgy of the Great Church: An Initial Synthesis of Structure and Interpretation on the Eve of Iconoclasm." *Dumbarton Oaks Papers* 34–35 (1982) 45–75.

———. *The Liturgy of the Hours in East and West: The Origins of the Divine Office and Its Meaning for Today* (Collegeville 1986).

Talley, Thomas, "From *Berakah* to *Eucharistia*: A Reopening Question," *Worship* 50 (1976) 115–137.

————. "The Literary Structure of the Eucharistic Prayer," *Worship* 58 (1984) 404–420.

————. *The Origins of the Liturgical Year* (New York 1986).

Vogüé, A. de, "Problems of the Monastic Conventual Mass, *The Downside Review* 87 (1969) 327–338.

Wilkinson, John, *Egeria's Travels to the Holy Land* (Jerusalem ²1981).

Winkler, G., "Confirmation or Chrismation? A Study in Comparative Liturgy," *Worship* 58 (1984) 2–17.

————. *Das armenische Initiationsrituale: Entwicklungsgeschichtliche und liturgievergleichende Untersuchung der Quellen des 3. bis 10. Jahrhunderts.* (OCA 217, Rome 1982).

————. "The Original Meaning of the Prebaptismal Anointing and Its Implications," *Worship* 52 (1978) 24–75.

Index

abbot, 22, 24, 25f., 40
Ad Gentes (decree on missions), 82
Ambrose, bishop of Milan, 47, 53, 54f., 62, 90
and eucharist as missa, 18
Andrieu, M., 78n.74
anointing, 47–48, 55, 57, 67
in capite, 61
in frontem, 61, 62, 63, 64, 67, 101
with myron, 55
Apostolic Constitutions (AC), 12, 21
dismissal structure of, 11, 16, 26
Apostolic Tradition (AT), ix, 5ff., 8, 9, 10ff., 19, 26, 27f.,
    32, 57, 60, 62, 67, 76, 92, 94, 95, 96, 106, 110
and anointing in frontem, 57
baptism as messianic anointing in, 51
baptismal rite in, 41ff.
bishop's baptismal role in, 45ff. 90, 91
epicletic prayer in, 44
exsufflation in, 6
hand laying in, 6
"Lord God" prayer in, 46
signation in, 6
Verona version of, 47ff., 57ff., 63, 65, 91, 118
Arians, 18
Athanasius, 61
Augustine, Saint, 15ff., 31, 53, 56
Austin, Gerard, ix, 27, 72n.10, 122n.39

baptism,
in Ambrose, 18ff.
anointing in frontem and, 57
in Apostolic Tradition, 5, 10–12, 21, 41, 44ff., 57, 58ff., 65f.
in Augustine, 15ff.
chrismation at, 52, 101
as "consignation," 5, 57
deferral of, 28
dismissal at, 3ff., 39ff.
in East, 8–10
in Egeria, 13ff.
episcopal oversight of, 54
imposition of hands at, 45
as missa, x, 46, 51, 57, 64
presbyteral chrismation and, 54, 63
rite of, for adults, 83
signation after, 42, 45
signation at, 6
signation of forehead at, 46, 51, 63, 64, 101
tactile and olfactory elements of, 102–103
as water bath, 51
in the West, 14ff. (See also: *coming to bishop's hand; dismissal; missa.*)

Barberini Euchologion, 52
Basil of Cappadocia, 60
berakoth, 7
de Bhaldraithe, E., 23, 37n.50
bishop, 6, 8, 9, 11–12, 14, 24, 31, 43, 44ff., 50, 53, 54, 56, 57, 61, 63, 68, 71, 92, 93, 96, 108
"blessing" of penitents, 16
Bobbio Missal, 48, 91
Book of Common Prayer (American Episcopal), 42, 112
Borella, P., 36n.38
Botte, B., 33nn.4,5,6; 34nn.15,16; 48, 73nn.12,15,16,18; 74nn.20,21,24,25,26,27; 75nn.33,34,35,36,37,38; 90, 99, 121n.27, 122n.32
Brightman, 34n.18, 36n.42

Caesarius, bishop of Arles,
and dismissal, 19, 20, 28, 30
Canons of Laodicea, 8f., 11, 19
Cassian, dismissal in monastic usage, 15, 20, 21, 25
Cassiodorus, 20
catechumens, dismissal of, 16, 18
Celestine I, pope, 20
Cherubikon hymn, 5
chrismation, x, 39, 52, 55, 58, 61, 91, 92, 95, 101
presbyteral, 54, 57, 91, 92, 94
Chrysostom, John, 61
Code of Canon Law (1983), 81ff.
on the sacraments, 84
coming under the bishop's hand, 15, 16f., 22, 28, 29,
    46, 51
confirmation, x, 3, 42, 65f.
anamnesis and epiclesis in, 104f.
as "completion" or "perfection" of baptism, 3
consignation as, 53, 65ff., 68
Dix's view of, 41f.
in Eastern churches, 65
education and, 102, 107f.
and epiclesis of eucharistic prayer, 54
grace of, 71
influence of AT on, 52ff.
Innocent I and, 52ff.
missa structure as basis of, 65ff.
in ninth-century Gaul, 68f.
origins of, 3, 4, 65, 69ff., 117
pneumatic character of, 95
Roman evidence of, 56ff.
as separated from baptism, 64, 68, 70f.
spiritual seal and, 55, 60
structure of rite, 42ff.
three-stage origin of, 65ff.
confirmation, reform of, 87ff., 106ff.
adult initiation and, 89f., 96

age for reception of 87, 88ff., 99–101
closer relation to baptism and, 96
and Byzantine rite, 92, 106
catechesis and, 107ff. 114f.
celebrated after baptism, 94ff.
chrismation and, 94f.
and Code of Canon Law, (1983), 84
eucharist and, 84ff., 114, 116–117
first communion and, 88, 112–113
and hand laying, 92–93
initiatory context of, 100
and initiatory reform, 82ff.
ministry of, 89, 93
penance and, 88
problems concerning, 101ff.
postbaptismal chrismation and, 90, 91–92
and reform of Christian initiation, 83ff., 96
and relationship to eucharist, 96f.
structure of, 93–94
Vatican Council II, and, 81ff.

consignation, x, 45–46, 52ff., 61, 64, 65, 68, 92, 94
missa structure as basis of, 65f.
of newly baptized, 56, 57
presbyteral, 63
*Consilium ad Exsequendam Constitutionen de Sacra
   Liturgia*, 82f., 89, 113
Constitution on the Church, 82ff.
Constitution on the Sacred Liturgy (CL), 81ff., 89, 106
Councils
of Agde, 25, 30
of Arles, 54
of Carthage, second, 15, 61–62
of Constantinople, 61
of Elvira, 54
Laodicea, 10, 11, 26
Milevis, 30
Nicea, 8
of Orange, 54, 55

Riez, 54

Vatican II, 81ff. 108, 113, 119

Cresswell, R. H., 34nn.18,20

Cuming, G.J., 33nn.4,5,6; 34nn.15,16; 73nn.13,16,19; 74nn.20,21,24,25,26,27; 75nn.28,33,34,35,36,37,38; 77n.61, 121n.22, 122n.40

Cyprian, 53

Cyril, bishop of Jerusalem, 12, 28, 52, 61

Dallen, James, 35nn.29,30

Damasus, pope, 15, 60

De Baptismo, of Tertullian, 90

Decentius of Gubbio, 56, 90

De Sacramentis, of Ambrose, 90

Didache, 8

Didymus, *On the Holy Spirit*, 60

dismissal

before communion, 27ff.

by bishop, 15–16

in Caesarius of Arles, 19

of catechumens, 9ff. 16, 18, 19, 20, 28f.

at compline, 22

at end of Word service, 19

at eucharist, 28f., 40

in Gallican liturgy, 19

hand laying and, 7, 10, 16, 26, 42, 54, 60, 61

in monastic liturgy, 20–27

of non-communicants, 29, 34, 40

as origin of confirmation, x, 34, 40

in Sozomen, 15 (See also *missa*.)

Divinae Consortium Naturae, (Apostolic Constitution of Paul VI), 90, 92, 106

Dix, G., 33nn.4,5,6; 34nn.15,16; 41, 48, 72nn.3,4,6; 73nn.13,16,19; 74nn.20,21,24,25,26,27; 75nn.33,34,35,36,37,38; 77n.61

Dölger, F.J, 34n.19, 35n.27
Dura Europas, 43

Easton, Burton Scott, 49–50
Egeria,
travels of, 12ff. 18, 22, 25, 28, 40
dismissals in, 13
missa, 13
Mohrmann's views on, 14
and "Prayer for All", 44f.
energumens, dismissal of 10–11, 16
prayers for, 20
Epiphanius of Salamis, 61
eucharist, 13, 18, 20, 23–24, 26, 46, 68, 81, 84–85, 86,
    87, 89, 96f., 99, 100, 106, 108, 110, 111, 113, 114,
    116–118
Eutychius, 5

Faustus of Riez, 67, 70, 90
Felix I, pope, 20
footwashing, 53, 54, 55
Fisher, J.D.C., 72n.7
Funk, F.X., 34n.18

Gamber, K., 38n.67
Gelasian Sacramentary, 47–48, 53, 58, 60, 63–64
Great Entrance, 5
Gregory the Great, pope, 31

hand laying, 6f., 10–12, 14–16, 27–28, 31, 41, 45, 48,
    50–51, 53–55, 57–58, 62, 67–68, 91–92, 94–95, 101–
    102, 118
Heinemann, J., 33n.10
Hilary of Poitiers, 61
Hispano-Gallic "confirmation," 55
holy communion, in monasteries, 22, 23

illuminated, dismissal of, 11, 16
Innocent I, pope, 52ff., 56ff., 62–63, 68, 70, 71, 106–107, 110
Institutes of Cassian, 15
Isidore of Pelusium, 61
ite missa est, 22

Jerome, saint, 56, 60, 110
John the Deacon, letter of, to Senarius, 53–54
John Chrysostom, 28, 29
Jungmann, J. A., 19, 20, 34n.22, 35n.31, 36nn.39,40,41,44; 72n.1

Kavanagh, Aidan, ix, 32n.1, 72nn.5,6
Kelly, J.N.D., 77n.65
Kilmartin, E. 38n.64
Kleinmyer, 121n.27
Krautheimer, Richard, 77n.57

Lampe, G.W.H., x, 47, 72n.5, 73n.27, 75nn39,40; 77n.61, 78nn.66,67
laying on of hands (See hand laying.)
Leo I, pope, 57
letter to Decentius (Innocent), 62, 63, 64, 68
Lindenbauer, B., 21, 36n.47
Lord God prayer, 47, 48, 51, 53, 58, 60, 61, 63–64, 69–70, 91
Lumen Gentium, 82

Macedonians, 60, 62
Marsh, Thomas, 27n.5
Mathews, T., 32n.2
McCann, J. 36n.46
Melchiades, pope, 67

missa
in Ambrose's writings, 13, 14, 18, 20
in Augustine, 15
as "blessing of penance," 16
in Cassian, 15
of catechumens and faithful, 16
confirmation as, 117
as dismissal ceremony, 20
in Egeria's travels, 13, 14, 18, 20
in monastic texts, 20ff.
of non-communicants, 29
as office, completed by prayer and hand laying, 20
and origins of confirmation, 41ff.
structure of, 40
in Western usage, 15, 16 (See also dismissal.)
Missale Gallicanum Vetus, 48, 91
Mitchell, L.L., 78n.72
Mitchell, Nathan, 71–72, 78nn.75,78; 80;
  122nn.33,34,35,36
Mohrmann, Christine, 14, 25; 34nn.23,24;
  35nn.27,32,34; 36nn.35,36,48; 37n.57
mystagogy, 63
De Mysteriis, of Ambrose, 90

Nicea, Council of (325), 8
Nicholas Cabasilas, 5

oblatio, 24
oils, 43, 44, 45, 46
Optatus of Milevis, 61
"orders" of Christians, 17

Paul VI, pope, 90, 91–92, 106
penitents,
dismissal of, 8, 9, 10, 11, 15, 16, 17
hand laying upon, 15
"Prayer of Inclination," 27, 29ff.

presbyter, 7, 15, 24–25, 41, 43–45, 50, 54, 61–63, 89, 92–94

Quinn, Frank C., 72n.2, 75n.32, 76nn.50,51; 77n.52

Rite of Christian Initiation of Adults, 84ff., 94f., 99
Rite of Confirmation, 102ff.
Roman Pontifical, 82–83
Roman Ritual, 83
Rule of Benedict (RB), 21ff., 40
Rule of the Master (RM), 21ff.

sacraments, as story, 116
Sacrosanctum Concilium, 81 (See also Constitution on the Liturgy.)
"sealing," 7, 8, 39, 41, 51, 55, 60, 62, 90
signaculum, 8, 9 (See also "sealing.")
Sozomen, dismissal in, 15
sphragis, 7, 8
spiritual seal, and postbaptismal anointing, 55, 60, 62
Steidle, B., 25, 37n.56
structural analysis, and liturgy, 65f.

Taft, Robert, 28, 29f., 33n.3, 36nn.48,49; 37nn.53,58,59,60; 38nn.63,65,69; 78nn.69,70,71
Talley, T., 33nn.9,10
Tertullian, 53, 55, 57, 62, 91
Theodor of Mopsuestia, 28

under the bishop's hand, 14ff.

de Vogüé, A., 22, 23, 24, 36n.49, 37n.52

Wilkinson, J., 34nn.21,25; 35n.34; 76nn.42,49
Winkler, G., 72n.6, 77n.56; 78nn.73,76
women, ordination of, 103